Smith

v.

Jones

Interesting Cases
In Magistrate Court

Robert F. Simms

ISBN: 978-0-9995929-8-4
Printed in the United States of America

To my father, Stewart B. Simms, Sr.,
who was always behind me,
and would have been happy
to see me pursue justice
from the bench.

Contents

INTRODUCTION

Even the most casual television viewer has noted that the most popular subjects for TV drama are doctors and hospitals, law enforcement, and courtroom drama. The reason is equally simple to discern. People's experiences when confronted with crises and challenges by definition make for the most interesting storytelling. Those of us who have been involved personally with real life drama usually have intense interest in the similar experience of others. Those of us whose lives are humdrum like to project ourselves into much more exciting daydreams. Life in Mayberry has a charm that sticks with us gently; but a glimpse of life from the dashboard of a police car in pursuit, from over the shoulder of a surgeon, or from the jury box of a solemn courtroom, grasps our attention and embroils us in the raw emotions of the characters who struggle for life itself.

In the few years that I have been on the bench as a county magistrate, I have marveled at how it seems that as interesting as things were yesterday, today's events in the courtroom are even more fascinating. And the magistrate court is certainly one of the best places to encounter the puzzling, engaging, bizarre, or heart wrenching drama of everyday life in the real world. I have sometimes noted that if all the freaky murder stories depicted on any of several top police dramas actually took place every week—as regularly as the episodes of the show—the news would be nationwide and the country would be riveted to their screens until the crime spree abated. But on a slightly lower scale of intensity, a weekly and even daily stream of routinely bizarre events takes place in magistrate courts—to say nothing of local police departments—across the country, and it's all happening under the noses of the largely unaware public.

Pick a court, any court, and attend it whenever it's in session, and chances are you will find it hard to get up in the middle of a case and leave. Especially is this true where civil matters are involved. That's a personal opinion, and I'm certain that judges who deal with criminal matters most of the time find the drama that swirls around those cases to be of greater interest than the squabbles of Joe and Jane Citizen that never involve the State as a party. Most of my work is with civil matters, and I have found them to be an endless source of interest.

Most civil disputes that wind up in court are just honest differences of opinion between two or more honest people, about money. An occasional character shows up who tries to perpetrate fraud upon the court, and more or less regularly someone who has no legitimate defense against a complaint will fail to tell the whole truth or nothing but the truth. Every once in a while someone will be engaged in his version of a disputed matter when the other party will blurt out, "Liar!"—but this is rare.

Actually, the only time I have raised my voice to a booming, command level in court was on such a rare occasion. A defendant was being cross examined by the plaintiff, who in response to one of the defendant's answers interjected some out-of-place, direct testimony in contradiction, to which the defendant, barely six feet from me, erupted spontaneously with, "J___ C___, holy M___ of G___!" He didn't delete the expletives, however. I punctuated his outburst with the most forceful two raps of my oversized gavel that have ever been heard in my courtroom, and in my best command voice I told him, "Sir, you *will* control yourself!" and he immediately apologized and calmed down. Court tends to evoke strong emotions. That's part of the reason it's fascinating.

In this volume, I present some of the daily drama of civil cases in my courtroom. It's not high drama: a subject matter jurisdiction of $7,500.00 for most case types keeps the stakes comparatively low. But the only courtroom most people ever see is the magistrate level court (justice of the peace, or small claims court, depending on the state where you live), and when it's you who are at one of the parties' tables, it will be very important *to you.*

A goodly portion of most tales in this book is taken up with the written Judgment I delivered in the case. Magistrate court in South Carolina is a Summary Court; it is not a court of record. Most judgments in summary courts are given off the cuff, I think, and forms in the computer systems we use enable a court clerk to simply choose "plaintiff" or "defendant" from a drop-down box, fill in a few blanks with dollar figures, and print the result for the judge to sign.

From the start, however, I decided to invest a bit more time in the process, for the benefit of both the parties and me. They want to know what facts I found, why I rendered judgment for or against them, and how I dealt with disagreements. At least, I think they do; I would. But the process also benefits me: I want to delve into the matter and articulate my thinking in a written Judgment. Writing is actually a part of my thought process, and when I can plainly state my reasoning and my conclusions, I am most confident in the accuracy and the justice of my decisions. Thinking realistically, I know that virtually no one outside the parties and me will ever read my Judgments, and there is no court below the magistrate court for which any of my Judgments would serve as precedent, but it satisfies me to write them all the same. And I think it helps the people who win or lose to know why.

I have tried to tell the stories with enough realism to be convincing while also engaging in some of the artificial sterility of legal language. I have minimized description that might resemble a novel while maximizing the precision of my own eyewitness testimony. Most of the chapters have been written while the cases were still fresh on my senses—a day after a trial, or even the same night.

All the stories are true, like the episodes of the 60s TV series *Dragnet.* And like those tersely written tales, in my stories the names have been changed to protect the real people described, a fraction of whose lives took place in the confines of my courtroom for all the world—or at least anyone who cared to come to court—to see.

My reason for obscuring identities is principally to elevate the narrative to a more pure, storytelling. There may be a vague and inarticulable motive on my part to avoid the remote possibility of personal animosity for my broadcasting people's private squabbles. After all, however, court records are public. Anyone can come by the court, ask to see a case, and inspect it or obtain copies of it. We are obliged to give access to open case files to local independent contractors who look for cases for the various TV judge shows. Consequently, the cases in this book certainly could have been recounted with the actual names, dates and places. Nevertheless, I have decided to let the characters wear masks.

I also could have written under a *nom de plume,* but then, I suppose I am sufficiently vain to want my name associated with my book.

The following facts have been obscured by the use of substitute names, phrases or numbers:

Parties – Each Plaintiff is Smith and each Defendant is Jones. None of the first names, where given, is actual to that particular party, either. Smith is the most common last name in the United States, and Jones comes in fourth.

Lawyers – I could have chosen among famous, actual attorneys—Darrow, Cochran, F. Lee Bailey, Gloria Allred—but I didn't want to prejudice the reader. I could have gone with Mason and Matlock, but those names might have evoked too many fictitious associations. When involved, are lawyers are Johnson and Williams. Johnson is the second most common last name, and Williams is the third.

Dates – References to years have been made with "last year," "the third year," or some other contrivance intended to give the reader a relationship to the present without specifying which exact year events took place.

Witnesses – When other persons testified, their names, too, have been made up. Most witnesses are named Green.

Places – While the author's location is readily discovered, I will give you no further help in identifying the cities or towns involved, though if you figure them out, you still won't have anything useful. Companies, too, are fictitious. Where the Plaintiff is a company, it is named for Smith, and the same goes for Jones.

I'm reasonably certain that once I have sent this volume off to the printer, I will want to add just one more chapter to it—the one that took place that very day. If I just wait another twelve months, I will probably have volume two on my hard drive.

May the reader enjoy these slices of real, everyday life as it unfolds, gets peeled back, cracks open, gushes out, and otherwise exposes itself in the polite wrestling match of the magistrate courtroom.

I
A No Win Situation

Sometimes plaintiffs do not prevail in court because they simply don't have a case. Sometimes they have a case but just don't make it well. When one or both parties are unrepresented by attorneys, South Carolina Rules of Magistrate Court direct the judge to question the parties in order to assure that all claims and defenses are fully presented. There is a fine line, however, between the judge's asking questions on the one hand to elicit the information he needs to make a decision, and his asking questions on the other hand that serve mostly to make a plaintiff's case, or a defendant's defense, for him. This is especially true when allegations are made in pleadings that are never made again at trial. In this case where a landlord sued his former tenant, follow-through from pleadings to hearing was crucial.

The Pleadings

Plaintiff Abby Smith filed suit against Defendant Kendra Jones asking damages in the amount of $7,500.00 for costs incurred in repairing and remodeling her townhouse rental unit at 10 Brown Way in Littleton, formerly occupied by Jones. Smith's complaint alleged that Jones failed to inform her of plumbing problems in the townhouse that resulted in extensive damages to the property. Specifically, she alleged: that Ms. Jones had not paid rent according to paragraph six of the lease; that Jones failed to notify Smith of a hot water problem with the upstairs bathroom and dishwasher, which resulted in extensive damage and cost to the property; that Jones abandoned occupancy of the property leaving the water running, causing further damage; that Jones made alterations to the property without written consent; that Jones did not keep the upstairs hall sink clear of clogs; and that Jones damaged the carpet and doors beyond normal wear and tear, broke closet doors, and caused a large hole in the stairway carpet.

To this litany of claims, Jones's answer was that she did give notice to Smith several times about the upstairs leaks and that Smith had not addressed the problems adequately. She said the damage resulted from the landlord's negligence in making repairs. She alleged that black mold was forming in the ventilation system. She denied leaving water running. She also denied abandoning the property, though she says she left mid-lease and gave the landlord the keys. She denied all other claims.

The Evidence

Plaintiff

At the hearing, Plaintiff Abby Smith began her testimony by presenting nine sheets of photographic evidence. Jones did not object to any of the exhibits. The Court, however, had to pull testimony out of Smith by repeatedly asking her what she wanted me to note in the exhibits. The first exhibit was a photograph of a jagged hole in the dining room ceiling, exposing floor joists from the second floor and showing significant water stains. Both parties agreed the ceiling had fallen through at this location. A few photographs, all digital and all printed on home printers, were beyond recognition, being fuzzy or impossible to locate. An under-sink view from the kitchen showed some water stains on shelf paper. A shot of the kitchen floor appeared to show a few laminate boards that may have been wrinkled. Plaintiff had torn up a board on what she said was the kitchen floor to show water stains on the sub-flooring. Some yellow stains Smith said were cat urine were pictured on a carpet in one place and some brown stains that Smith identified as having been caused by pet feces were pictured on carpet in another place. (This testimony struck the Court as credible.) Another picture showed a bathtub dripping. Again and again, the Court asked what the Plaintiff wanted me to notice. Mostly Ms. Smith just stated the obvious—"it's a stain; I don't know what it is." And later, "you can see where the floor is warped," when I didn't see what I would have described as warping.

I did not take it to be my role to construct a series of questions to elicit testimony from the Plaintiff that would make her case for her, so at some point, I simply let the matter go. Plaintiff then introduced a copy of the lease, with little comment except to identify the pet addendum on the back and to state that the cat had caused damage. What damage, she didn't say. The one picture purporting to show a hole in the carpet was extremely fuzzy. The image contained nothing helping to establish what may have caused it, and Smith added nothing by way of her own testimony. Smith did state that she kept the Defendant's deposit of $770.00 but that it didn't begin to cover the damage. The Court asked if she had ever sent Jones an accounting of her use of the deposit, and she said no.

Smith then presented for the Court's inspection an estimate from Acme Construction Co. for remodeling the townhouse. I informed Ms. Smith that an estimate is inadmissible unless the maker of it is present to testify. Initially discombobulated, Smith then clarified that the document was not only an estimate, but a contract, and that she had paid Acme to do much of the work on the estimate. Since she could testify to what she herself paid and what she saw done, the Court allowed the document for those purposes and asked her what she wanted me to notice about it. She pointed to the section on replacement of hardwood, which described work to the kitchen floor.

Although the Court asked her several questions that would give her the opportunity to elaborate, Smith didn't give further evidence that might serve to prove that the replacement of the kitchen floor was necessitated by any negligence of Defendant Jones. In fact, while she had the entire kitchen floor replaced, she didn't have any work done to the base of the cabinet underneath the kitchen sink, which—if a leak from that sink were the cause of the kitchen floor damage—would certainly have needed replacing. I finally just listened while Smith went from one vague allegation to another. It was like a game of connect the dots where the dots were indistinct, not plainly made, and didn't finally form any particular pattern.

Jones declined to ask Smith any questions, and Smith called another witness, her brother Ryan. Ryan said he came to the townhouse in response to Smith's call a little more than two years ago, after Smith had received a call from Jones saying she thought there was a leak upstairs. Ryan looked at the fixtures in the upstairs bathroom and thought they might be loose. He said sometimes fixtures leak and you don't see the water, that it goes down through the walls. He tightened all the fixtures and left.

Six months or so later, Smith asked him to return to the townhouse. This time Ryan took his uncle Don (Smith's brother), a handyman that Smith had used before. The Court asked if either of them was a licensed plumber or contractor. No. Ryan volunteered that Smith occasionally asked him and Uncle Don to take care of things in her properties "to save some money."

On this second visit, Ryan noticed the ceiling bowing—which he said was what Jones complained of—and he went upstairs and changed the faucet washers, as well as the cold water stem in the bathtub, which he said probably had been leaking. Then he went downstairs, got a few pieces of 2 x 4, and propped up the ceiling with them, telling Jones he would return in a few days to remove them. He did return, when he believed the ceiling would have dried out (although he did not testify about whether or not it was wet), and he removed the boards and left.

Again, Jones had no questions, and Smith had no more witnesses.

Defendant

Kendra Jones had been waiting her turn patiently. It had seemed to the Court that there were cross examination questions she would have wanted to ask, but when I asked her if she were sure she didn't want to ask any questions, she smiled and said she would just wait.

Jones told the Court that in her first year in the townhouse, three years ago, she had complained to Smith by phone and by email that she could hear what sounded like running water behind the tub wall in the upstairs bathroom. She described the common sound one hears in a house when a faucet somewhere is on, just barely. She could not find a faucet on. Jones said Ms. Smith sent her brother (this was apparently Ryan's first visit two years ago) to take a look. She didn't know what they did on that occasion. She only knew that she still thought water was leaking somewhere.

In another few months, she called Smith again with the same complaint. Jones confirmed that Ryan and Uncle Don came to the townhouse, and she was appalled when they left after replacing some washers and putting in boards just to prop up her ceiling. She continued to hear the running water sound. It was only a few days after Ryan removed the boards that Jones came into the house one night after work to discover that the dining room ceiling, right where the boards had been, had fallen through.

Jones called her father, who advised her to leave. She said she gave Smith a thirty day notice and then moved.

Smith declined to ask any questions of Jones, even any questions designed to test the truth of Jones's claims of having called and emailed her about possible leaking water. When the Court had given each side an opportunity to add anything to their testimony, thinking certainly that one or both of them would contest or contradict the testimony of the other, neither one did, and the Court retired to deliberate. I returned with the following findings and Judgment.

THE JUDGMENT

The Court makes the following findings of fact upon a preponderance of evidence:

1. Tenant Jones informed Landlord Smith of a plumbing problem at least three times (I gave dates from the testimony). On each occasion, Jones's notice gave information adequate to inform Smith that a potentially serious plumbing issue was developing. Smith, however, did not seek professional help and service. Smith's sending her son and brother, "to save some money," was an inadequate response.

2. Under § 27-40-440(2) of South Carolina Law, the landlord's obligation is to "make all repairs and do whatever is reasonably necessary to put and keep the premises in a fit and habitable condition." Smith's failure to take sufficient steps to fully remedy the plumbing problem upstairs at 10 Brown Way in Littleton bars her recovery for the property damage that resulted. That portion of her Complaint that involved the damage to the upstairs bathroom and the dining room below, therefore, is dismissed.

3. Smith's inspection of the property yielded photographic evidence of various damage throughout the townhouse. In addition to the damage from water, Smith noted numerous carpet stains and holes that came from pet activity. The Court finds that these damages were beyond the scope of normal wear and tear. However, the Court heard no testimony about the age of the carpet or its expected lifetime. The Court is left with no means to determine if the carpet was due for replacement anyway. In the absence of such evidence, the Court cannot make a finding as to the cost of repairing just the stains and holes, or as to whether or not those stains were capable of being cleaned, or as to whether or not the Tenant must bear the entire cost of the replacement of the carpet. The Court must dismiss that portion of the Complaint that involved damage to carpets.

4. Smith testified that Jones had allowed a leak under the kitchen sink to damage the cabinet and floor underneath and had never told her about the condition. Jones did not contradict this testimony and the Court finds Smith's testimony credible. Smith further alleged that the water damage under the sink was the cause of slight warping of laminate kitchen flooring at what appeared in photographic evidence to be six to eight feet away from the sink. However, the evidence was insufficient for the Court to make any finding that a causal relationship exists between the two. The amount of monetary damages that might be due Smith for the property damage under the sink, however, is entirely uncertain. Smith paid $7,350.00 to Johnson

Repair Co. for work performed under "Item 3" of its contract with her. Included in that item was "Demo[lish] water damaged kitchen floor and damaged underlayment; Install vapor barrier;" and other items that may have peripherally involved the under-sink area, though nothing is specifically mentioned about work directly underneath the sink. The stated repairs were done to the entire floor, and Smith could offer no breakdown of the costs. The Court has no guidance whatever in determining damages to the area under the sink, leaving the matter entirely to speculation, in which the Court will not engage. Unable to determine monetary damages, the Court must dismiss this portion of the complaint.

5. While Smith also alleged in the Complaint that Jones made unauthorized alterations to the property, left an upstairs sink clogged, and damaged closet doors, she gave no testimony at trial upon which the Court may make a finding of fact, and these complaints are dismissed.

6. Finally, the Court notes that while Smith may have been able to recover some monetary damages from Jones if sufficient evidence thereof had been provided to the Court, Smith's losses were already offset somewhat due to her having $770.00 of Jones's money in the form of a security deposit. Smith testified that she did not return Jones's security deposit to her and made no accounting to Jones for any amounts deducted from it. §27-40-410(a) of the South Carolina Code of Laws (1976) as Amended requires that "Any deduction from the security/rental deposit must be itemized by the landlord in a written notice to the tenant together with the amount due, if any, within thirty days after termination of the tenancy and delivery of possession and demand by the tenant, whichever is later." §27-40-410(b) states that "If the landlord fails to return to the tenant any prepaid rent or security/rental deposit with the notice required to be sent by the landlord pursuant to subsection (a), the tenant may recover the property and money in an amount equal to three times the amount wrongfully withheld and reasonable attorney's fees." However, while the

law states that the tenant *"may recover,"* it is the responsibility of the tenant to assert this claim before the Court. Jones did not assert this claim, and the Court makes no award to Jones.

There being no finding of monetary damages that can be awarded to the Plaintiff, the Court renders Judgment for the Defendant.

During the reading of the Judgment, Smith had suddenly become alarmed at being told about treble damages for failing to give a written accounting of her use of the security deposit, and I noticed that she appeared to be thinking that not only was she not going to recover damages from Jones, but she might walk out owing Jones more than $2,000.00. She was relieved to hear otherwise, however, and between her disappointment and her relief, she left looking nonplussed.

2

BUSINESS OR PERSONAL?

Litigants who file and conduct their own cases sometimes do not know how to caption their suits. A *pro se* litigant may file a case against a person instead of his business. Occasionally, if the person runs a one-man business, the case may be re-captioned to correct the name of the defendant as late as the hearing of the case, and no harm, no foul. But every once in a while, the names of parties become really important. In this landlord-tenant case, things got "curioser and curioser" as the Court questioned whether the matter was business or personal.

THE PLEADINGS

Mitchell Smith was a man known to the Court, a middle aged fellow of affable and easygoing demeanor who tended to let people take advantage of him, the polar opposite of his father, who had been a shrewd businessman. Smith filed to evict Randall Jones in June, stating that he and Jones had a lease for a property at 300 Main Street, and that Jones had not paid rent in ten months. Smith also checked the box on the form stating that "the lease term has ended." Immediately after the papers were served, Defendant Jones called the court to protest. He said something to the effect that there was another person in the picture and that it wasn't all his fault. He further stated that he and the Plaintiff-landlord had a payment arrangement for the rent. Since no written Answer is required in an action for ejectment, Jones had only to request a hearing and bring his case to court—that, and pay any alleged rent.

The Court held Jones to the letter of state law, which requires that if a tenant whose landlord has filed to evict wishes to have a hearing, he must pay any alleged rent, or else show receipts to the Court proving he had already paid the rent. Further, he must continue to pay rent through the date of the hearing. (The legislature created this statute to prevent tenants from delay while waiting for trials, meanwhile missing further rent payments.) In the event that the amount of rent itself was in dispute, the Court could have a rent-only hearing to decide that issue so that the proper amount of rent could be paid. Since the amount of rent was not certain to the Court, a rent hearing was scheduled in this case.

Meanwhile, Smith filed a separate suit over the back rent, a Summons and Complaint for $7,500.00, the jurisdictional maximum for the Magistrate Court. Few details were given in the Complaint about how Smith arrived at the figure. What was curious about the suit was the caption. The court's clerk knew that Smith had filed the suit, but the caption of the Summons and Complaint was Smith LLC v. Jones. The suit was over the same lease situation, but now Smith was suing in the capacity of his company.

In his Answer to the Summons, Jones provided the Court with a copy of the lease at the root of the two cases. The lease was between Smith LLC and Jones Inc. Six years ago when the parties entered into the lease, Smith had signed for his company and Jones for his, along with a second person, a Mr. Green. In his Answer, Jones hinted that Green was the other person involved on his side and stated that he should be named in the suit as well, if things were to be fair.

The Court reviewed the Pleadings from both sides carefully in preparation for a rent hearing on the eviction action, and the court clerk scheduled both cases for the same date so that in the event that the rent due were paid, enabling Jones to have a hearing on the merits, both cases could be heard as a convenience to the parties. They agreed to the plan.

The Court, meanwhile, arrived quickly at a decision as to whether or not the two cases could go forward at all.

THE EVIDENCE

At the hearing, both Smith and Jones appeared unaccompanied by any other person, including the phantom Green. The Court had marked the lease in the pleadings as Court exhibit 1, and began by asking both Smith and Jones if they recognized it. Both agreed it was the lease, and agreed that their signatures appeared on page 10, the signature page, on behalf of their respective companies. But Smith said it was missing a page. Which page, the Court inquired? Page 11, said Smith, the Personal Guarantee. This bit of information was a revelation, for the lease provided by Defendant Jones, not having had any personal guarantee page, had previously suggested to the Court that Smith's Summons and Complaint was improperly filed against Jones personally when the lease was with his company. I had entered the courtroom that afternoon expecting to dismiss the Summons and Complaint. This new revelation changed my course.

With these preliminary questions answered, the Court made a ruling:

Mr. Smith improperly named Mr. Jones as defendant in the Application for Ejectment from the commercial property at 300 Main Street. The lessee on the property is not Mr. Jones personally, but Jones Inc. This is a business lease. Two persons acting as principals of Jones Inc. appear to have signed the lease. The only way the Plaintiff can eject the business entity from this commercial property is to file against the business, not against an individual connected with that incorporated business.

A further difficulty exists with the ejectment action, however, that is perhaps more fatal to the action than naming Mr. Jones personally. Mr. Smith has listed himself as the Plaintiff. Nothing on the Application for Ejectment itself would indicate that this was an action between two businesses, but the court exhibit shows that the property is the subject of a lease between Smith LLC and Jones Inc. Mr.

Smith is a principal in Smith LLC. However, Mr. Smith has no lease with Mr. Jones. Mr. Smith therefore lacks standing to bring suit against Mr. Jones for possession, or even against Jones Inc. had he named that business instead.

The distinction is vital. Mr. Smith cannot recover personally a debt owed to his business. The Court is not inclined to amend casually the captioning of the case to reflect changes in either one or both parties as named. The only proper way for the matter to be handled is by a re-filing, if Smith LLC wishes to do so. In the case of the Defendant, in fact, re-filing would be demanded, so that, among other things, the business, Jones Inc., would have the statutorily required time to respond to the action.

The Court therefore dismisses the Application for Ejectment against Mr. Jones.

As to the Summons and Complaint, it appears that it may go forward, in light of the probability of the Plaintiff's introduction of evidence showing that Mr. Jones personally guaranteed the debts of Jones Inc.

Plaintiff

With the Summons and Complaint left to be heard, the Court swore in both parties and took the Plaintiff's testimony. Smith made things short and simple. His LLC, which included family members of his, rented the property on Main to Jones's company six years ago and until early last year Jones Inc. had paid the rent regularly. Then Jones defaulted.

Smith revealed that Jones and he were good friends and had been for quite a while. Because of this personal connection, Smith had enough information about Jones's business to know that things were bad, and he allowed Jones Inc. to pay less rent than the lease called for, for a period of several months, and still be considered paid in full. But then Jones defaulted even in paying this amount. However, after a few months, business was better, and Smith and Jones worked out a plan for Jones to catch up the back rent. Unfortunately, these payments were erratic and then stopped. Smith filed for ejectment when it was clear that Jones was not going to keep his bargain.

Smith now moved into evidence his copy of the lease, including the Personal Guarantee page, and he testified that the page obligated Mr. Jones personally for any debts of his company arising out of the lease. Jones did not object to the exhibit.

Defendant

Jones had a minor question in cross examination that didn't address anything relevant. But for his defense, Jones brought up the whole matter of Mr. Green, saying that Green had been loosely partnered with him in his business, having co-signed the lease six years ago, as well as co-signing the personal guarantee. However, as Jones further testified, Green was not actually a partner or employee of Jones Inc. This new information made the Court wonder why Green would have signed a personal guarantee, but then, Jones himself said he didn't remember signing the personal guarantee, and tried to cast some doubt about whether or not the signature on that page was his, though the Court, upon inspecting the signature, had no doubt that it was.

Jones continued to answer the questions the Court was thinking:

- Why had Smith not filed against both Jones and Green? —Green had dissolved his own business and was living with his parents, unemployed and "judgment proof."

- Did Smith currently have an action against Green, who apparently had left Jones holding the bag? —Smith had not filed suit against Green, but certainly will now.

Jones added that his own company had been dissolved through forfeiture, but that he had not done it himself, that Green had, and without Jones's permission. (Jones continued to operate a business, obviously as a "d/b/a.")

■ How had Green been able to act on Jones's behalf in filing with the Secretary of State to dissolve Jones Inc., when Green was not even part of Jones Inc.? —Jones wanted to know that himself. The Court privately developed another thought, namely that Green probably should be charged criminally with some kind of fraud.

All this was interesting, but not specifically relevant to the case at hand. The fact is that Smith had chosen to file suit against Jones only, that Jones had personally guaranteed the rent owed by his company, that the company was in default, and that the total back rent owed was now $14,000.00, as Jones was still in the property. Smith waived any amount over $7,500.00. (He didn't have to. As long as Jones was in the property, the jurisdictional limit did not apply: the statute does not place a dollar limit on landlord-tenant damages in such cases.) With no more testimony to be given, the Court was ready to render Judgment, when Defendant Jones made an additional statement that further complicated things. As he had done now and then during the testimony, he turned to Smith—the two appeared to be on relatively good terms—and he asked him when something Smith had alluded to took place: was it before or after Jones had begun *living in the property?*

The Court's ears pricked. Do you mean, I said, that you currently live in the property? Yes, Jones said. The Court knew the property was originally a residence on Main Street, and that most of the houses along that stretch had been zoned residential/business in recent years. When, I asked, did you move in? Jones had moved in perhaps a year after his business leased the property. Did Smith know Jones intended to live there when the lease was signed? No. Did the lease contain any agreement for Smith to use the house as a residence as well as a business? No. Did Smith, once he had knowledge of Jones's living in the property, make any sort of verbal agreement with Jones about living there? No. Was Jones therefore not paying any rent on the property to live there as well as work there? No.

The Court was ready to render Judgment in the Summons and

Complaint but began by first addressing the matter of the judicial dismissal of the Application for Ejectment, the eviction case previously disposed of:

THE JUDGMENT

1. First, the revelation that Jones Inc. is dissolved introduces an interesting twist. Since Jones Inc. does not exist, legally, being dissolved, Jones Inc. cannot be evicted. The Court previously stated that Smith could re-file if he wished, naming the parties properly as Smith LLC and Jones Inc. However, in light of the new evidence, Smith cannot evict the business named in that way. Yet Jones is still in the property, since he moved in as a resident. Since there exists no landlord-tenant relationship between Smith LLC (or Smith the individual, for that matter) and Jones the individual, Smith cannot file an Application for Ejectment against Jones, since that action is based on there being a landlord-tenant relationship and rent being paid.

I paused before going on, because I sensed that for me to continue by instructing Smith that what he wanted to file was an action for Summary Ejectment of Trespasser, I would be giving Smith attorney-type advice, and in open court at that. Instead, I stated that if Mr. Smith had further questions, he could pose them to the clerk of the court after the hearing. The clerk was well trained in how to explain the types of suits available to litigants without advising them to file or not to file any particular one.

Having thoroughly done away with the eviction action, finally, the Court was ready to render Judgment in the Summons and Complaint, which was truly simple:

2. The Court finds wholly for Smith LLC and orders Mr. Jones to pay Smith LLC $7,580.00, which includes costs.

Both parties thanked the Court and went out having polite conversation. They continued to chat in the courtroom lobby for nearly a half hour, long enough for me to prepare the Judgment and for the clerk to hand each of them a copy. Before they left, they both appeared at the window while Smith picked up the forms for Summary Ejectment of Trespasser against Jones. Then they left together.

ROUND TWO

Smith didn't file the forms, at least not right away. No doubt because of his personal connection to Jones, he let more than six months expire, hoping that Jones would vacate on his own. He didn't.

Finally, Smith appeared at the courthouse, caught my attention from the front window, and told me, "Judge, he's not leaving. I hate to do it because we're friends—in fact, he's probably my best friend—but I have to have him out and he's not going on his own." I asked him if he had filed the Notice to Quit. Since he hadn't done so previously, he was now going to file both a Notice to Quit against Jones personally and an eviction against Jones's business—making certain that Plaintiff and Defendant were named properly on each suit. The summonses were served and a hearing was held.

At the hearing, the parties again appeared to be getting along amiably. The case was cut and dried: the eviction was a simple matter of nonpayment of rent, which the Defendant fully admitted; the summary ejectment was equally simple in that the Defendant did not have a landlord-tenant agreement and the Plaintiff wanted him to move. Mitchell Smith would be glad for Randall Jones to both work and live there if he paid rent. Defendant said, however, that at present he was unable to pay either rent for his personally residing in the building or rent for his company to exist there. He expected to be able to do so any day, however, when his ship came in—a ship in the form of a judgment against a company he had sued for more than $10 million.

The Court was quietly dubious that Jones's expected windfall was shortly, or ever, forthcoming; however, the Court merely asked if the Defendant knew if he would be able to pay what he had admitted he owed anytime soon. He did not know, and he had no other defense.

I rendered Judgment perfunctorily for the Plaintiff on both the ejectment of Jones's company and the ejectment of Jones and his various family and friends who had accreted into a large and varied household by this time. They would all have to go. In giving my decision to Jones, I was as friendly toward him as Smith had been, and Jones nodded, having known it was coming.

Smith left the courtroom and proceeded to the office window and paid for the Writ of Ejectment. After it was posted, the Court did not hear from Smith about his needing a set out of either Jones's business or family. Two weeks later, the clerk inquired of Smith and learned that Jones had come up with some money (amount not disclosed by Smith) for both tenancies and Smith was satisfied. The cases were closed.

I had no doubt that Mitchell Smith had taken far less than he was owed and probably would continue to do so, until his property taxes on the formerly upscale residence, now a business property increasing yearly in value, exceeded his income in rent. Then he would be back, apologetically filing against his best friend. Or, perhaps Jones's ship would finally come in.

3
LAWSUIT IS BREACH OF CONTRACT!

Most of the time, a lawsuit is filed *because* of a breach of contract. Occasionally, the lawsuit *is* the breach of contract—by the party bringing suit. Here's a case where going to court was a good reason to do just that: go to court.

THE PLEADINGS

Patricia Smith petitioned the Court for Judgment against Mary Ellen Jones, in the amount of $1,400.00, on the basis of a Promissory Note signed by both parties by which Jones, who was buying a car from Smith, would pay Smith beginning in April 10 of one year and would continue monthly payments until retiring the debt in April of the next year. Plaintiff Smith asserted that Defendant Jones had made no payments at all. Smith filed suit on April 22, the same month the first payment had been due.

Jones Answered that she made two payments on or before the dates due, sending them by mail to 400 Mill Creek Road, Bigtown, an address she claims Smith gave her at the time the two agreed to the terms of the Promissory Note. She further Answered that Smith violated the contract by making demand for payment in full prior to the due date of April 10, one year after the first payment, and by failing to give her notice that payment was not received, which Jones argued was "required by law."

Interestingly, Jones filed a Counterclaim. She claimed that Smith had misrepresented the car and had failed to tell her about a door problem which, she alleged, resulted in injury to herself. Jones claimed extensive medical bills as damages. In a continuing litany of cross-complaints, Jones said Smith had invaded her privacy, attempted to defame her by addressing her as "Rev." in correspondence (!), which somehow at the same time called into question her minister's licenses. She said the lawsuit was defamatory, substantially false, implied malice, etc. After throwing in a few more references to her credentials as a minister, a counselor and a mediator for the family court, she cobbled together a few phrases normally associated with claims for negligence, breach of contract and even criminal conduct, and asked the Court for $38,000.00.

Because the Counterclaim exceeded the jurisdictional limit of the Magistrate Court, the case was automatically transferred to the Circuit Court. After a few months, it came back. Attorneys for each side had agreed to the dismissal of the Counterclaim entirely, with prejudice. The case was remanded to the Magistrate for trial as originally filed, but without the Counterclaim. I had read the Counterclaim and consequently had already gotten the flavor of the Defendant's personal constitution; however, sworn to be impartial, I determined to take no cognizance of the Counterclaim in hearing the case on its merits.

THE EVIDENCE

Plaintiff

At trial, Smith told a story laced with folksy details about how she had met Jones, who had expressed interest in a late model Lincoln that Smith had for sale at her home. Both ladies were in their seventies, and had socialized a bit over tea before deciding to do business. On the day of the deal, Jones was accompanied by her elderly husband Joe.

The two women drew up the Promissory Note, which stated, apparently for information purposes only, that the sale price of the Lincoln was $13,400.00 and that Jones had already secured a loan through her bank for $12,000.00. The Note was actually for $1,400.00, the remainder, and Smith said Jones agreed to pay it off in monthly installments by the tenth of each month, to be paid in full by April 10 of the following year. The Note then continued: "The balance is interest free and no demand shall be made for payment in full prior to the due date as set April 10, [one year later]."

Plaintiff Smith then stated simply that she didn't receive the first payment, that she attempted to call Jones about it, and that there was no answer. She said she believed Jones intended to get out of paying the additional $1,400.00 for the Lincoln entirely, and that she decided to file suit because of that belief.

In support of her suspicion of Jones's intent to not pay the $1,400.00, Smith testified that Jones had originally offered her $12,400.00 for the Lincoln, that Smith had held firm on her asking price, and that Jones had been reluctant to agree to a Promissory Note for the difference.

Defendant

In her defense, Jones told a rambling tale of her visits to Smith's property, their dickering about the car, and their final agreement. Jones said she had made the first payment by mail and she showed the court an envelope addressed to 400 Mill Creek Road, Bigtown, which had been returned as being a bad address. She mailed the payment to that address because, as she stated firmly, Mrs. Smith had told her that she actually lived on Park Road, but because the traffic was so bad there, she put her mailbox around the corner on Mill Creek, the side road, and that Jones should mail her payment to 400 Mill Creek Road.

Before she had gotten the envelope with her first payment back from the Post Office, and before knowing that she had already been sued for defaulting, Jones had mailed May's payment to the same address, and she presented that envelope and the two checks she had enclosed in them. In fact, the second letter was unopened, and the Court opened it and verified that it contained the May check.

Inspecting the two envelopes, the Court also noted, though silently, that the return addresses were different. They were not pre-printed but appeared to be done on a computer printer at the time the addressee was also printed. I jotted down an observation and then testimony resumed.

Even after being served with Smith's suit for the entire $1,400.00, Jones made two more payments, one for June and July for $233.00 and one for August and September, also of $233.00, attempting to stay up to date with the agreed monthly installments. By this time, she had gotten another address to use, and she presumed that because the letter didn't come back, Smith had gotten it. She moved into evidence a carbonless copy of the two money orders from her bank. She found out eventually—during the previous year while the Circuit Court had the case—that her bank had voided the money orders when they had not been cashed, and had credited back to her account the $466.00.

Smith attempted cross examination but seemed intent on testifying instead, and the Court directed her to wait until an opportunity for rebuttal.

Jones then called her husband Joe as a witness. Joe stared at me when I called his name to come to the stand. He had not heard me, but when I raised my voice slightly, he did, and he took a seat in the witness box. I made a mental note.

Joe testified that he had been with his wife Mary Ellen the day of the actual sale and that he heard Patricia Smith say what his wife said she did, about mailing payment to 400 Mill Creek. The Court directed a few questions to Joe Jones. The witness box was right next to the bench and Joe was only about six feet away, but when I spoke in a normal voice, he didn't hear me. Mrs. Smith volunteered from her table that Joe didn't hear well. Joe had no other testimony to add, and I soon dismissed him.

Given the opportunity for rebuttal, Smith said that she had received the two money orders but that on the advice of her attorney (while the Circuit Court hearings were going on) she did not negotiate them but retained them pending the outcome of her suit.

Both parties wanted to say more, and had attempted to, throughout the hearing, but it was mostly petty bickering and irrelevant to the Court, though it was no doubt relevant to the two scrapping women. The allowable testimony completed, the Court deliberated and then issued the following Judgment.

THE JUDGMENT

On a preponderance of the evidence, the Court makes the following findings of fact:

1. Defendant Mary Ellen Jones made her first two payments to Plaintiff Patricia Smith in good faith. The Court cannot conceive of circumstances under which Smith would have given a wrong address for Jones to use in mailing payments. However, it is reasonable for the Court to conclude that Defendant Jones, or her husband, who has substantially impaired hearing, did not hear the address correctly when given to her at Smith's residence.

2. Jones's two letters bearing the first two payments bore different return addresses for herself, neither of which had a proper ZIP code for her own mailing address. The return address for the first envelope said, "Mary Ellen Jones, Paralegal-Civil/Family Court Legal Mediator, PO Box 555, Bigtown" and bore a ZIP code for nearby Littleton, one of three ZIP codes actually assigned to that small town. The second envelope said, "Mary Ellen Jones, Paralegal-Civil Court Legal Mediator, PO Box 555, Bigtown, and had one of the other ZIP codes for Littleton. Bolstered by the observation that Mrs. Jones presents inaccuracies in listing her own address, the Court finds that Jones was mistaken about Smith's mailing address but also that she did mail the payments in good faith, as the exhibits make abundantly clear.

3. Jones made two subsequent payments for the third and fourth months and the fifth and sixth months in good faith, even after Smith's lawsuit had been filed against her.

4. The inclusion of the provision in the Note that Smith could not make demand for payment in full until April 10, one year after the first payment, essentially gave the nature of a term loan to the Note, even though the Note also set up monthly payments. In effect, the Note, as a contract, prohibited any penalty for late or missed payments, or any action taken to enforce the contract at all, until the termination date.

5. Smith's filing suit in this Court just twenty-two days after the first payment was due was a material breach of the terms of the Promissory Note. Had Smith made a demand in writing to Jones that did not involve the Court, the demand would not necessarily have been found to be material, if it had not led to any damages to Jones. The demand, however, was not made between the two parties, but using the auspices of the Court, and was made in violation of the terms of the Promissory Note, by which Jones should have been able to be assured that until the term of the Note, which was April 10, a year later, she would not have been liable for the entire debt and would not have been liable to civil suit for that debt. It is the filing of this Summons and Complaint, embroiling Jones in defense of an action in court, which made the early demand material.

6. In consequence of her demand's being made before allowed by the Promissory Note, Smith did not have grounds to file the suit. Irrespective of the fact that at the date of today's hearing, the term of the Note has now passed and the balance of the amount due on the Note has become due, the suit was filed at a time and under circumstances not supporting the Plaintiff's right to file.

Based on the finding of this Court that Smith filed suit without sufficient grounds to do so, and on this finding alone, the Court renders Judgment for the Defendant, Mary Ellen Jones, without prejudice to any other issue between the parties not herein adjudged, and dismisses the Complaint.

The Court deliberately left open the issue of whether or not Jones would pay Smith the $1,400.00 now that the term of the Note was expired. Word on the street was that Jones did not pay it, that Smith reluctantly dropped the matter, and that both ladies went back to having tea with their other friends.

4
PARSING A POWER BILL

An Affidavit and Itemization of Costs, a sworn statement that sets out the exact amount owed by a defendant—liquidated damages—makes for a simple case, most of the time. But then there are those Complaints that ask the Court to decide what is a fair figure for damages when there is no invoice and no testimony available as to just what a complainant actually paid or lost when he was treated unjustly. The judge must take what evidence he does have, and do what judges everywhere charge juries with doing: use those faculties of common sense all human beings use to evaluate the evidence. The case of a former tenant seeking equity from the Court illustrates the principle.

THE PLEADINGS

Plaintiff Samantha Smith sued Jerry Jones for $1,825.00 for excessive heating and air conditioning costs from March through January of her second year of tenancy at 100 Prettygood Lane. Smith's Complaint was a rambling paragraph alleging extremely high bills and an inattentive landlord. Jones's Answer denied he did anything wrong and said he would come to court to hash it out.

THE EVIDENCE

Plaintiff

Smith testified that she began renting from Jones two years previous to the trial, during the winter. Smith was about twenty-five and transmitted very quickly the impression that she was naïve about a number of matters, not the least of which was what it took to run a household. On this subject, in fact, Smith said once or twice that she had never rented a house before and didn't know what to expect in the way of expenses. Her first power bill in the house—which was a seventy-five year old two-story with eleven rooms—was for more than $500.00. She said she was shocked, but didn't know that $500.00 wasn't typical, and she paid it and didn't say anything. When the next month's bill was for more than $600.00, however, she called the utility company.

The utility company sent a service person who checked her meter and verified that the bill was correct. He didn't give her any further help.

Smith testified that she emailed Jones about the high bills and how cold the house was and other little problems with the house she wanted him to fix. She said that he generally dismissed the owner's responsibility for repairs and told her that one of the reasons she got the house for as low rent as she did was that she agreed to assume responsibility for fixing things. She said he also told her that her power bill may have been high because of her Christmas lights.

When spring began to arrive, Smith's bills got lower, but with the onset of summer months they went up again and she said she registered another complaint in July about the temperature in the house. She said in fact that she gave notice to Landlord Jones at various times during that same year that "the temperature was not what it should be," and that Jones would not address the issue. Her testimony at the hearing made it clear to the Court that she hadn't used the term "HVAC" or "heat pump" with Jones, at least at first.

Tenant Smith wrapped up her testimony by fast forwarding to January of her third year, when Jones agreed, after Smith's continuing complaints, to allow her to move out at the end of February because of high power bills, without penalty for ending her lease early. By then, landlord Jones had taken action on the HVAC problem, having a professional repair the ducts underneath the house and replacing a burned out element in the heat pump. Tenant Smith learned about the burned out element from the repairman himself. (The Court tolerated this bit of inadmissible hearsay, both because the Defendant did not object and because it really did not serve to prove any material fact.) This repair took place in mid January.

Smith said she got another fairly high utility bill for January and that in more discussions with Jones, he had made overtures about possibly rebating some money for her previous, high bills. She moved out at the end of February, tried to talk with Jones about his offer, and said he didn't want to discuss it anymore. It was then she decided to sue.

Defendant

In his defense, Jones made a few short statements and offered no documents into evidence. As to offers he made to rebate some money to Smith, Jones said he had made such an offer in general terms, but that when Smith moved out, she began talking about figures in the several thousands of dollars, and that he cut off any discussion of the matter at that point. He said she told him she would sue, and that he said, "Do what you feel you have to."

Backing up to tell his side of the story, Jones said he had gotten no notice of a problem with the HVAC system until November of Smith's second year of tenancy, and that it wasn't until December that he got more specific information from Smith, whereupon he called in a repairman. Jones said he graciously allowed Smith out of her lease because she was so unhappy. He stressed again that he would have acted sooner if notice had been given sooner.

Samantha Smith was certainly no lawyer, but she knew enough to wave a sheaf of emails she wanted to present to the Court and to ask if she could present some more evidence. The Court instructed her to make her statements into questions for cross examination and she could introduce the documents during that time. She moved into evidence various emails she said documented notice to Jones early during the first year of her tenancy. The Court inspected the emails and found that they actually documented notice beginning in July of her second year. In the emails, Smith was overly polite about making direct and specific complaints about anything other than minor matters. The emails appeared to be avoiding the kind of insistent, complaining approach that Smith thought would upset her landlord. But come July of that second year, she accompanied a plumber looking at a leak under the house, and together they made a startling discovery.

In rebuttal testimony, Smith explained to the Court that "the things that connect the vents to the air conditioner" —meaning the flex ducts in this case—were not connected at all. She gathered up her courage and reported directly to Landlord Jones in a July 3 email, "The air conditioner was running under the house—cold under there like in the air conditioner ... the back room has nothing coming form [sic] the vents and the den either." This statement should have constituted sufficient notice to the Landlord that a significant problem existed with the HVAC system that required immediate attention. Smith added that she went around the house with the plumber and noticed at his direction that cold air was coming out of all the external vents to the crawl space. To a question by the Court as to whether or not the vents had louvers in them, she said no.

The Court then asked Ms. Smith what basis she used to calculate her claim of $1,825.00. She had no documents and no specific figures she had computed. She did have her power bills for the relevant months, and presented them to the Court saying only that she thought her claim was a fair amount to recoup.

With the testimony and documents in hand, the Court recessed to deliberate, and returned with the following findings and judgment.

THE JUDGMENT

The question before the court is what damages the tenant has that can be recovered under law, specifically Section 27-40-610(b), which reads as follows:

Except as provided in this chapter, the tenant may recover actual damages and obtain injunctive relief in a magistrate's or circuit court, without posting bond, for any noncompliance by the landlord with the rental agreement or Section 27-40-440.

Regardless of whether or not Tenant Smith exercised her remedy under the law to end her lease if Jones failed to repair the HVAC issue, Landlord Jones was not at liberty under the law to ignore notice of the issue. The Landlord-Tenant act states in § 27-40-440(a) that "Landlord shall ... maintain in reasonably good and safe working order ... heating, ventilating, air conditioning." Nor can the Landlord refuse to make such repairs or conduct such maintenance by virtue of a rental agreement specifically excusing him from duties required under the Act.

Consequently, the agreement between Landlord Jones and Tenant Smith, testified to by both parties and documented in the emails, to the effect that the owner of the property reduced the rent on the condition that Smith would be responsible for miscellaneous repairs, is an agreement that cannot be used to support any contention that a problem with the heat pump system, whatever it might have been, could be ignored under the law. Once notice was given on July 3 that air from the HVAC was "running under the house—cold," the Landlord became liable for damages resulting from negligence in repairing the unit.

Upon a preponderance of the evidence, then, the Court finds the following:

1. A duty of care exists on the part of Landlord Jones under the law, and Landlord Jerry Jones was negligent in maintaining the heating, ventilating and air conditioning system, beginning with his notice in writing on July 3 of last year.

2. The Court is then left to determine from the evidence what damages the Tenant incurred from the negligence. The testimony of Tenant Smith was that her bills during the summer and winter months, when the heat pump ran regularly, were consistently high, although she did not know what electric bills should be in a house, since as she testified she had never rented a house before. Ignorant of what may have been a normal range for an energy bill for her house,

particularly one of eleven rooms as the house had, Smith endured the costs, becoming alarmed in December of her first year at how high the costs were, and beginning to sound that alarm to the Landlord in July of the next year. Her suit asked for one half the costs of her power bills for March of last year through January of this year, on her theory that she was probably paying double what she should have.

3. The Court has found that Landlord Jones had sufficient notice of the HVAC defect beginning July 3 last year. Consequently, the Court dismisses damages claims for the March, April and May power bills. The energy bills in evidence show that readings were taken about the 22nd or 23rd of the month. For July of last year, the date of the meter reading was approximately two weeks after Jones had notice of the HVAC defect. Had Jones corrected the defect within fourteen days as directed by law, essentially none of the June-July energy costs could have been charged against him; therefore, the bill for June-July, which was not listed as a claim by the Plaintiff anyway, is dismissed. Plaintiff's claims for damages will be considered beginning with the September bill from last year and including bills for November, December, and January of this year. Plaintiff provided no information about any bill for October of last year.

4. The January bill from this year was affected by the fact that the heat pump defect was repaired on or about January 5, about halfway into the billing cycle. Therefore, the Court will consider damages for only half the January bill for $304.48.

5. According to her own testimony, the Plaintiff's claim of one half the amounts of her energy/electric bills is not based on an exact or even approximate estimate of what were or may have been normal energy costs for her specific house during any month of the year. She testified to there being on her bills an indication of what the bill was for the same period one year previously, but she had not brought those bills to court as evidence, only a summary of her costs, which did not include the previous years' figures. In fact, even with such figures, no

way would have existed for Smith to determine what portion of her monthly bills was due to the defective HVAC system. Neither can the Court merely speculate as to what the cost would have been had the heat pump been working correctly at all times and been connected correctly and securely underneath the house.

6. However, the Court is not left with mere speculation. First, the evidence shows that during the months from at least July 3 of last year through January 5 of this year the heat pump was air conditioning and heating the crawl space under the house, and that the air being forced into the crawl space was also escaping liberally to the outside through the external vents on the home, which had no louvers on them that could be opened or closed. It is evident to the Court that this produced a situation in which the HVAC was running most of the time when temperatures were even moderately cold or moderately hot. From the evidence that the duct work not only leaked but that it was entirely disconnected from the vents in the crawl space and pumping air directly out of the house:

7. The Court finds it to be a reasonable conclusion that at least seventy-five percent of the heat pump's operation for September, November, December and January was due to the defect in the duct work and/or a burned out element that was ultimately found in the unit on or about January 5 of this year.

8. Further, it is common knowledge that HVAC costs are about half the energy costs of an average home. The Court therefore reasonably finds that half the amount of the Plaintiff's monthly bills was for the operation of the HVAC system.

9. To calculate the damages, then, the Court adds the bills for the period of September through half of January (excluding October), which total $1,255.09. Applying the Court's finding that half of that amount was due to HVAC costs, $627.55 was affected. Applying the Court's finding that 75% of that amount was due to the defect, the Court finds that the defect cost the Tenant $470.66 for the months Landlord Smith was liable for the defect.

Judgment is for Plaintiff Smith for $550.66 plus court cost.

Considering that he had been sued for $1,825 to begin with, Jones figured that getting out of court for less than a third of that was reasonable, and he paid it with a check before leaving the courtroom.

5
SUMMER VACATION OR SOMETHING MORE?

Most Notice to Quit actions are, if not cut and dried, at least easily determined, and more than seventy-five percent of them in this Magistrate's experience never involve a hearing. The trespasser simply moves. The following Smith v. Jones case did not follow the typical pattern.

PLEADINGS

Sue Smith filed for a Summary Ejectment of Trespasser against Jane Jones. A summary ejectment—a Notice to Quit—required no express complaint except what is already on the standard form, namely that Jones was on Smith's property without her consent and had not complied with a demand to leave. Jones submitted an answer to the court along with her request for a hearing. She alleged that Smith did not own the property, that someone named Green did, and that she had a lease with him. Jones demanded her day in court.

THE EVIDENCE

Sue Smith's sister Ellen accompanied her to the hearing. Sue Smith herself was a somewhat sullen young woman of slight build and a husky voice, about twenty five years old. Smith's demeanor immediately seemed indicative of something more than being upset over not getting the house back. Sue Smith's sister was a slightly younger, stocky girl with a detectably bitter attitude. Jane Jones was a slender, energetic woman of about twenty two who exuded the frightened determination of a survivor. The evidence of both parties filled in the story.

Plaintiff

Presenting her complaint, Smith testified that she had lived in the rental house belonging to landlord Frank Green for several months. She offered into evidence a copy of several pages of her lease, which did not include the signature page. Continuing, she said that with the onset of warm weather, she decided to move in with her boyfriend at a lake property for the summer.

> Smith mentioned this boyfriend only once, and appeared to rush away from the subject as if she hadn't meant to bring it up. Her later testimony was inconsistent. The Court developed the suspicion that things had not gone well with the boyfriend, cutting short her cohabitation with him, and that she needed to get her house back in a hurry. There being no further evidence to support this theory, and a finding of fact being unnecessary concerning it, the Court did not pursue the matter or make any reference to it in the Judgment.

Ms. Smith said her plan was to return at the end of the summer months. While she was gone, however, she wanted to sublet the house to someone else.

Sue's sister Ellen was acquainted with Jane Jones and knew that she needed a place to live. Jones, Sue said, was escaping a bad marital situation. While Smith was describing this situation, Jones began vigorously shaking her head "no" for the Court's benefit. Smith continued, saying that sister Ellen made the arrangement with Jones to take over Smith's lease payments for the summer, and said that when she told Mr. Green about it, he had no problem with the arrangement.

The Court stopped Smith before she continued reporting Green's words because there appeared to be no person in the courtroom who might be Mr. Green, and there was no attorney for either side to object to hearsay evidence. Smith said she returned earlier than she had thought, around August 1, and asked Jones to leave, but that she wouldn't. Smith added that Jones also had some of her—Smith's—property in the house and wouldn't give it to her.

The Court, hearing this curious testimony, asked Smith what property she meant. A television and another small piece of furniture, she said. What, asked the Court, happened to the rest of her belongings? Smith said she had it all moved out. Why? Because, as she said, she wasn't going to let someone else live in her house and use all her things. The Court began to develop the idea that perhaps Smith's "summer move" was not quite as she represented it.

Upon a question or two by the Court, Smith revealed that she had put her household things into a storage unit. The rental of a storage unit for barely three months and the significant labor and truck rental involved in emptying the house seemed to the Court to contradict Smith's claim that she was merely on an extended summer vacation.

Smith accused Jones of having told lies to Mr. Green to get him to agree to drawing up a lease with her—revealing to the Court that she knew that such a lease existed. Jones began to argue back across the aisle, but before the accusation could turn into a brawl, the Court called the parties into order and asked if Smith was finished with her testimony. She said she was, and the Court asked if Jones wished to ask her any questions. Jones wanted to make statements, and the Court made certain Smith had no more witnesses, and then turned to Jones for her defense.

Defendant

Jones, a rapid firing speaker, began to tell a different tale. She said she met Smith through Smith's sister, it's true, but that she wasn't trying to escape a bad marriage. In fact, her husband lived with her in the new location. Sue Smith never told her she could live in the house only for the summer—why, she asked, would she even consent to such a thing and move all her belongings there for three months? Instead, she said that Smith wanted to move but didn't want to have a problem with her landlord Mr. Green by breaking the lease in the middle of the term, so she was trying to arrange a transfer of the lease instead. Everything she told Jones indicated that the move was permanent.

Parenthetically, she said that the television was not being used and that Smith could have it, but not by coming over with gangs of other people and making threats, which is what she said Smith had done when she, Jones, would not move out on August 1. The two women again began bickering across the aisle and the Court had to interrupt a mounting clash.

When things were calm again, Jones continued. She said that Mr. Green had decided to draw up a lease with her instead of Smith because he said Smith had broken her lease. The Court interrupted again to instruct Jones not to report Green's words, because it was clear that Jones was trying to prove her contention that she had a legal right to live in the house by giving hearsay statements from the landlord. Jones said she had asked Green to come testify, and that she had talked with him earlier and he said he was driving in from a nearby county, where he worked (although he lived four houses away from the rental property).

Both sides offered some comments to the effect that they wished Mr. Green were there, and both sides believed Green would verify their side of the story. Green, however, never appeared.

Jones continued, offering into evidence a piece of notebook paper with a handwritten lease on it, signed by her and Mr. Green and notarized. She said she had to have a lease to get the utilities put in her name, which she had done on June 16, about two weeks after moving into the house. The utility company accepted this proof of her rightful occupancy and transferred service to her name.

The Court realized that Ms. Smith had not testified to anything regarding utilities, and that the implication of Jones's testimony was that she and Smith would disagree on how, why, and when the utilities were transferred to Jones. The Court reserved its own questions on the matter for the moment, thinking that the hearing might have to be continued.

Jones said that when Smith returned and demanded that she leave, it was the first she had heard about any idea that Smith's exodus was only for the summer. Smith had become almost violent with rage that she wouldn't leave, and Jones warned her that she would seek a Restraining Order against her.

With things heating up again in the courtroom and the testimony at an impasse, the Court devised a plan. Since it was already 5:00 p.m., the Court informed the parties that not only did the Judge want to eat supper, but also there was testimony lacking that the Court needed in order to make a judgment. Rather than rush to judgment with what evidence was in the record—and the Judge believed he knew which way it might go—the Court was going to continue the case until the next week, while it subpoenaed an additional witness. The Judge wanted to hear from Mr. Green.

To Be Continued

In fact, the Court subpoenaed Mr. Green and Ms. Glenda White, an employee of the utility company who had testified several times before in the court in eviction cases. By the end of the next day, the court's constable had served the two persons with the subpoenas.

When the hearing reconvened the following week, at the time set, Plaintiff Smith and her sister were present, and Ms. White was in the gallery, but Defendant Jones had not appeared. Neither, in fact, had Mr. Green. The clerk called the name of the Defendant at the courthouse door in compliance with the state statute, and there was no answer. The Court announced that the hearing would continue in her absence. Though I could have applied a court rule permitting a finding for the Plaintiff when the Defendant failed to appear, I chose not to. I wanted to hear the testimony of the additional witnesses as planned. Fortunately, while Ms. White was beginning her testimony, Ms. Jones came in hurriedly with her children in tow, who apparently had delayed her.

The Court had prepared a series of questions for both Ms. White and Mr. Green. Ms. White testified that Ms. Smith had fallen behind in her utility payments and was actually scheduled for a disconnect of her power on June 15, and that Smith called that very day to request a voluntary disconnect. White's notes of the contact showed that Smith stated that she was transferring her lease to Jane Jones, who would be putting the power in her name, and that she, Smith, wanted to make certain it wasn't turned back on in her own name. The utility company performed the disconnect. White also said the company later applied Smith's utility deposit to pay part of her unpaid bills, but that she still owed money to the company.

White said the company demands strict proof of a person's legal right to possess a property, meaning a copy of a renter's lease must be shown. Having seen and made a copy of that lease, the utility company put the power in Jane Jones's name. The Court asked if either party had any questions for Ms. White, and neither did, so the Court excused Ms. White.

By this time, Mr. Green had still not appeared, and the Court noted that fact and let it be known for the record that Mr. Green would be dealt with by the Court itself for his refusal to obey the subpoena. On the record, the Court said it had reason to believe that Mr. Green was deliberate in his disobedience and that by refusing to come to court on either occasion, he had made himself unavailable to testify.

Considering Mr. Green unavailable as a witness, the Court considered hearsay testimony about Green's statements to be admissible under the exception for unavailability. I told both parties I would allow limited, relevant testimony from each one as to what Mr. Green had told them about the lease and the sublease arrangement. Smith said Green told her the sublease was fine with him, and that since Smith had not finished paying him the deposit, he would get the rest of it from Jones in her first month's rent.

The Court asked Smith about any deposit she made on the rental unit, thinking that Green may not have returned the deposit or accounted for it as required by law. Smith said the lease did require a deposit and that she was supposed to pay half of it with the first month's rent and half with the second month's rent. She had not paid the second half. In testifying that Mr. Green had told her upon her leaving that he would get Ms. Jones to pay the rest of the deposit, she clearly, though inadvertently, indicated to the Court, out of her own mouth, that Mr. Green believed that Smith was leaving for good. Otherwise, he probably would not have required *Jones* to pay the rest of *Smith's* deposit, and Jones would not have consented to do so.

For her part, Jones said that Green had the same understanding that she did, that Smith's departure was for good. She added, "He said that Sue Smith had broken her lease and so he was going to draw up a new one with me."

The Court asked Smith if she had told Mr. Green the nature of her move. After some hemming and hawing, she said she had not. In other words, had she not given him a forwarding address? No, she had not. Smith wanted to add, and did, that her "summer move" was to join other family members at lakefront property. This seemed inconsistent with her earlier testimony that she moved in with her boyfriend.

At this point, the Court asked if either party had additional testimony that was not merely a rehashing of what they had already said. Somewhat reluctantly, each said she didn't. The Court then recessed to deliberate and returned with the following findings and judgment.

THE JUDGMENT

The Summary Ejectment of Trespassers action requires the Plaintiff to prove three things: 1) that the Plaintiff owns or has legal possession of the property in question; 2) that the Defendant is in or on the property without permission of the legal possessor and is therefore trespassing; and 3) that the Plaintiff has demanded the Defendant quit—or leave—and the Defendant has refused.

The Court looked very carefully at the first question: at the time of her filing for this Notice to Quit, did Ms. Smith have legal right to possess the property at 2400 Country Road.

The preponderance of the evidence submitted by all witnesses leads the Court to conclude the following to be facts:

1.   Plaintiff Sue Smith's exhibit of a lease between her and Frank
     Green lacks a signature page but I have no reason to believe it
     was not valid at the time it was created or that it was not legally
     signed. According to the evidence the Court finds credible, Ms.
     Smith had legal possession of the property under the lease at
     least from her entry onto the property in late March until the
     first of June of this year.

2.   Ms. Smith determined to vacate the property on or about the
     first of June. While she indicated in her testimony that she
     planned to move to family lake property with numerous other
     persons and that she planned to return at the end of the
     summer to 2400 Country Road, she also moved almost all her
     belongings out of the property, arranged for someone
     else—Jane Jones—to take over her lease (with the approval of
     Mr. Green, as both parties agree), and had the utilities
     disconnected from her name, stating to the utility company
     that she wanted to make sure that the power was not cut back
     on in her own name. At the time this took place, Smith was in
     default on her payments to the company, which ultimately
     applied her deposit to partly pay off her outstanding balance.
     All these actions of Smith suggest a move that was other than
     a summer absence.

3.   By arrangement between the parties, Jane Jones took up
     residence in the property on or about the first of June. Ms.
     Smith had her power disconnected voluntarily on June 15,
     which was on or about the date her power was scheduled for a
     disconnect for nonpayment of her bill. On the following day,
     the utility company connected service to the property in the
     name of Jones, upon her showing of sufficient evidence of a
     lease with Frank Green, the landowner. This series of events,
     which the Court finds to be factual, indicates that Ms. Jones
     had legal possession of the property on that date.

4.   The documents the Court has in evidence show that Mr. Green
     terminated his lease with Ms. Smith upon her leaving the
     property, removing her belongings and transferring the lease.
     He established a new lease with Ms. Jones as of June 16. It is

clear that the utility company determined by documents shown to them that Ms. Jones had lawful possession on June 16.

5. The Court must therefore find that Ms. Jones had proper possession of 2400 Country Road when this action was filed.

The Summary Ejectment action therefore fails.

***

OFF THE RECORD

The Court went off the record after the gavel came down, and addressed the parties.

> I am under no illusions that my judgment in this case will settle the entire disagreement between the parties. However, I had a single, simple matter before me, and I was limited to deciding on the application for Summary Ejectment only. While I am fully aware that Ms. Smith disputes the validity of Mr. Green's actions, that matter is or would be the subject of an entirely different suit, if Ms. Smith wished to file it. Respectfully, Ms. Smith, you may wish to consult an attorney about the matter.

At this point, it was Smith who began vigorously nodding up and down, and she left the courtroom vowing to get a lawyer and sue Mr. Green. The Court had its own day with Mr. Green, who was ruled into court to show cause why he disobeyed the Court's subpoena. Green actually appeared for the hearing, and denied having received the previous subpoena to testify. He said the only summons he had received was the Rule to Show Cause requiring him to come to this present hearing. The Court had brought its constable in to testify, and the constable, while he could state under oath that he had served the subpoena to testify to the residence of Mr. Green, could not swear that he gave it to Mr. Green himself, only that he gave it to someone of "suitable age and discretion" at the residence, which the statute on personal service allows.

The Court decided that in the absence of compelling evidence to the contrary, it could only conclude that this person of "suitable age and discretion" had not followed through by giving the subpoena to Green. I let Green go.

UPDATE AND ENCORE

About a year later, Jane Jones's name came up again in a court filing as a defendant. This time the plaintiff was Frank Green. Jones had not filed suit against him, and neither had Smith, for that matter. Green was still Jones's landlord. Apparently she had continued to live in the rental house and had paid rent, at least until recently. Green was filing for eviction for nonpayment of rent. Jones wanted a hearing.

Because Jones alleged in her brief answer that the amount of rent was uncertain, I granted a hearing to determine whether or not rent was owed, and how much.

At trial Green stated simply that Jones had not paid the last three months rent. Green had to use an interpreter much of the time. He was not a native English speaker and was in fact not a citizen of the United States. The Court previously suspected that Green had not appeared in the first case involving Smith v. Jones because he was possibly not even in the United States legally. I suspected that he was afraid of getting entangled in a legal matter and being found out. I had no grounds upon which to question him in this regard, so I didn't. His behavior, however, previously and on this occasion, suggested that he had not been in the States long and not only didn't speak English well, but was operating out of an entirely foreign basis of understanding the rights and responsibilities of both landlords and tenants in the United States.

Green had no written lease with Jones, as the Court had previously determined. Jones didn't take over Smith's previous lease, just payments for rent. But the handwritten notes Green provided Jones the previous year did not even specify the amount of rent Jones would owe. If that had been the only contractual basis for Jones's tenancy, the Court wouldn't have an agreement to enforce for rent. Fortunately for Green, he and Jones had signed another handwritten note between them four months ago in which Jones agreed to pay $600.00 per month in rent. Then three months ago she stopped paying that. For Green, that was the bottom line.

For Jones, it was merely a launching point for her to talk about mold-stained carpet, an inefficient air conditioner and other things. She had had the carpet removed and the floor redone at her own expense and complained that Green would not reimburse her or credit the amount against her rent. So she withheld rent, hoping that would prod him to act.

I asked Green if he had given Jones written demand for rent or he would begin eviction proceedings. He had not. Since there was also no lease, there was no other notice in writing that Jones had been given of this demand. While an intelligent person realizes if he doesn't pay his rent, he deserves to be evicted, the law requires that written notice be given. If that notice is not in the lease, the law requires a separate written demand for rent and notice of eviction if it is not paid.

This technicality—but an important one—allowed the Court to rule in this way:

> Mr. Green, I don't know how they do things where you come from, but in this country the law demands certain things of both tenants and landlords. One of them is that a landlord give a five-day, written notice to a tenant that if he or she does not pay rent, he may be evicted. I have determined that you have never given that notice. On that finding, I must render judgment for Defendant Jones and dismiss your petition for eviction.
>
> Ms. Jones, before I dismiss court I advise you that nonpayment of rent is what I call a deal-breaker. The law

allows you to purchase essential services and deduct the cost from the rent when the landlord is negligent in providing them, but essential services are narrowly defined in the law and I didn't hear anything suggesting you were within the definition. You simply cannot withhold rent in order to force a landlord to do something.

Your remedy under the law is first to give Mr. Green a 14-day notice demanding that either he will fix substantial problems or that you will leave the property without penalty for early termination of lease. In your situation, that wouldn't be a danger anyway, since you don't have a lease. Under no circumstances I can think of would the Court assist you to stay indefinitely at a rental home without paying rent, just because the landlord did not do what you asked.

That said, your other remedy under law is to sue Mr. Green. If you have monetary damages from the landlord's negligence, you would have to file against him to recover. I'm not advising you *to* do anything, just informing you *how* you would need to proceed if you did, in order to be within the law.

Further, I need to inform you that if even now Mr. Green were to give you written notice and then file for eviction again, in order to have a hearing in defense on the issues you have brought up today or on others, you would have to pay Green the rent allegedly due, or pay it into the Court, which would hold it pending the outcome of the case.

Mr. Green, I am not advising you *to* give Ms. Jones a five-day notice, just informing you that if you wish to file eviction against her for non-payment of rent, you will have to give her that notice. I am, however, advising you to go educate yourself on what landlords in this state must do in order to be in compliance with the law.

As the parties rose to go I noticed that Ms. Jones had become pregnant since the previous year's case. Her perhaps eight month fetus would probably make his or her debut in this world at a different residence, and from what I had seen, that was a good thing.

YET ONE TIME MORE...

All was not over, however, as one month later Mr. Green appeared to file eviction papers against Ms. Jones. This time Green had a copy of the letter he had delivered to Ms. Jones about two weeks after the previous hearing. He gave her the required five day notice. It had been almost two weeks since, and now Green wanted to get Jones out.

The court generated the Rule to Vacate or Show Cause which was served on Defendant Jones. Seven days later, on a Friday, Jones came to the courthouse window. She claimed that she had been out of state for a few days for a death in the family and had found the Rule to Vacate on her door when she returned. Her ten days would be up the following Monday, but she denied having even been at home when the court's records said she had been served. As often I do when a question about valid service arises, I just reserve the defendant and start the count over. It saves appeals down the road for lack of jurisdiction. In this case, the Constable simply went out to the house and served Ms. Jones later that afternoon.

However, while she was at the courthouse window that Friday, she insisted that Green would not accept the payment of rent, that he avoided her, and that he said he just wanted her out. She was angry that he had given her the notice and then not allowed her to pay.

I had to inform Ms. Jones that Mr. Green did not have to accept her rent but that even if he did, he didn't have to cancel the eviction proceedings. I explained to her that the law allows a landlord to collect what he is owed but still evict for late payment. She didn't think that was fair. I explained to her the reason for the law was to protect the right of landlord to evict for habitually late tenant payment of rent without having to file subsequent suits to recover amounts owed. She still didn't think the law was fair, but she wasn't finished. Jones wanted a hearing on the eviction.

I didn't think I would hear anything different from what she had told me at the previous hearing, but I was obligated to give her a hearing *if* she qualified. Another part of our landlord-tenant law requires tenants who want hearings on eviction proceedings to pay all rent allegedly due before the Rule to Vacate, and to continue to pay rent until the matter is determined at trial. I told Ms. Jones that I would schedule a hearing as soon as she paid the rent due. In this case, since Green was refusing to accept rent, Ms. Jones could bring me a money order or cashier's check for the amount of rent now due—$1,800.00—and I would grant a hearing. She had ten days from the date of service of the Rule to Vacate to make this payment and qualify for a hearing.

Naturally, Jones didn't like this law, either. Again, I gave a brief explanation of the reason for the law, trying to avoid putting it bluntly. The blunt version is simple: the legislators wanted to protect landlords from tenants who use requests for hearings, especially jury trial requests, as tactics to delay the inevitable, when in fact they have no valid defense against the eviction—they simply can't pay the rent. The more tactful version I gave Ms. Jones was clear, but it didn't satisfy her.

If she really had money in hand to pay Green the rent, she would have had money in hand to pay that rent into the court, but in fact, she didn't. I had little doubt that she simply did not have the money for the rent and would not be able to come up with it by ten days from then. I explained to her that if she paid the rent into the court and she prevailed at the hearing, the rent might be returned in part or in full to her, but that if she did not prevail at the hearing, the money order or cashier's check would be given to Green. Her face told the story. She didn't have the money and she wouldn't come up with it, because she realized she would lose it. Her request for a hearing was simply a delay tactic. If I were wrong, I would gladly admit it, but I didn't expect to be proven wrong.

In spite of what her facial expressions had told me, Jane Jones repeated to me the conditions: "So I have ten days to pay $1,800.00 to you, and I can have a hearing?" This was where the date of service of the Rule came into play. Since I had decided to take her word for it that she had not been served properly with the Rule, she had ten days from that day to pay her rent into the court. I confirmed the timetable, and she left the courthouse with the bearing of a victor. I did not expect to see her in the next ten days. The only think she had won, as I believed, was another ten days in the house.

Defendant Jones did not prove me wrong. When the ten days lapsed, Green returned for the Writ of Ejectment. The Constable, as eager to be done with this case as I was, posted the Writ that day. The following day, we scheduled a set-out. It was not necessary, however. Knowing that her time had finally run out, Jones had gotten the help of a few friends and had moved her things out the previous day and into the night—to where, I had no idea.

I hoped, of course, that Jane Jones would be able to avoid eviction proceedings ever again. I noted privately that I had never heard anything more about the husband she had claimed, during the previous year's hearing, lived with her in the rental house. I believed that he probably didn't live there anymore; if he had, certainly I would have seen him with her at some point in her contest for possession of the house. Accordingly, I hoped that Jones would get her feet on the ground, get a job and make a stable and peaceful home for that baby that was not going to be *in utero* much longer.

Realistically, however, and sadly, I was prepared to see her name on another eviction filing a year or so down the road. Unfortunately, I have just come to recognize the pathology when I see it.

6
THE FASTER I GO, THE BEHINDER I GET

Companies engaged in the deferred presentment of checks, commonly known as payday lenders, are legal businesses in some states. These businesses enable people living from paycheck to paycheck to borrow several hundred dollars for a few weeks, at what—if calculated at an annual rate—would be 300-400% APR. Because the state allows and regulates such business by law, a court case involving a payday lender as a plaintiff cannot result in the court's finding that the legal rate charged is unconscionable, no matter how much such confiscatory rates offend the conscience.

Such is not always the case with other contracts, however. It is possible for a contract to contain provisions which, though agreed to by both parties, may be unconscionable for one reason or another. The question was raised in the Court's mind by the evidence in this Summons and Complaint over a matter of back rent.

THE PLEADINGS

Smith filed suit against Jones for unpaid rent from December of one year and January and part of February of the next year. In his Complaint, Smith said that Jones had begun renting from him in August, paid each month until December, and then defaulted. Smith claimed he had evicted Jones in February, and that Jones owed him back rent and late fees for December, January, and a portion of February. In addition, Smith said Jones had not transferred utilities into his name, and that Smith had finally paid Jones's past due utility bill in order to get the power turned back on for another tenant later. Smith's total claim of damages was $7,500.00, the subject jurisdictional limit of this court.

Jones's answer was that he and Smith had an arrangement whereby he would catch up on back rent by paying $300.00 per week until the debt was settled. But, he said, Smith went ahead and evicted him in February. Jones alleged that he tried to stop the eviction by calling the magistrate while his possessions were actually being set out of the rental property, but to no avail. He implicitly admitted he owed some money to Smith, but not as much as Smith claimed.

THE EVIDENCE

Plaintiff

At the hearing of the case, Smith, a professor of computer science at a local university, testified that he leased the rental unit to Jones beginning in September of the previous year. His first exhibit was a copy of the lease, which showed the lease term beginning September 1. A date of August 19 appeared on top of the lease and on the signature page. The signature page also showed both the Plaintiff's and Defendant's signatures, and the lease appeared to be in good order. Smith quickly summarized the story as he had in his Complaint: Jones paid each month through November. November's payment was late, but Smith allowed it without penalty because Jones reported that he had lost his job. When December's rent was not paid by the 5th, however, Smith contacted Jones, who said he still was not employed but hoped to be in a few weeks. He promised payment by the following week. When that week came and went, he called Smith to promise payment in yet another week.

Smith began sending Jones payment coupons that he constructed just for that purpose, as a reminder to Jones to pay, and having lines to fill in the amount of rent and the amount of penalty being paid. Smith then told the Court that he reminded Jones that the penalty for late payment was 10% of the unpaid rent balance per day, as long as a balance was outstanding.

The Court's eyebrows were raised (inside my head) at the results of rapid mental calculations going on of how much penalty Mr. Jones began to rack up beginning December 6. Smith's Complaint had not contained the actual per-month rent Jones owed or how much, if any, Jones had paid in deposit. Jones's Answer, however, had stated that his rent was $900.00 per month and he had made a deposit of $850.00. The Court could see the dollar signs multiplying against Jones.

Smith continued that he proposed a plan in early January whereby Jones could make up the $900.00 he owed for December, and the $900.00 that had just come due for January, by making weekly payments of $300.00 until the base rent was paid. Jones had just come upon a job that paid weekly, and he agreed to the plan. Smith said Jones made two weekly payments and then didn't pay him anything more, and that as a result, when Jones defaulted on rent for February, Smith filed to evict him.

The Court noticed that a key part of the Plaintiff's claim must have been left out of the testimony, namely the exact amounts that Jones owed as of the date of his ejectment from the rental unit on February 17. The Court wanted to know, and asked the Plaintiff directly, if the daily penalty of 10% of the unpaid rent continued and would continue to mount up during the time that Jones was trying to pay off his rent in weekly installments. Smith said it would and it did. He pointed out that the lease stated very clearly that the tenant would be charged 10% of the base rent due, after the grace period, which was the fifth of the month.

How much was the bottom line, the Court wanted to know? How much did Smith say Jones owed him for the two and a half months of unpaid rent plus a utility bill of about $700.00? Smith looked down at his notes and rattled off a figure well over $15,000. Since he had been advised that the most he could ask for in Magistrate Court for a Summons and Complaint was $7,500.00, he filed for that amount without giving the details in his Complaint.

Eyebrows now fully raised (still internally), the Court asked Mr. Jones if he had any questions for Smith. Jones was a median adult whose speech and conduct suggested that he was lacking in education. He didn't understand the process in the courtroom and began testifying instead of cross examining. The Court asked if he would like to go directly to his own testimony, and he nodded.

Before allowing Jones to present his case, the Court asked Mr.

Smith casually if he had any documents relating to the eviction. Smith at first said he had the letters he had sent Jones about payment and telling him he would be evicted if he did not bring his account up to date. The Court repeated its interest in seeing copies of the eviction papers or receipts for an eviction action filed with the court. No, he had not brought any such records. Noting that fact for possibly raising later, the Court turned to the Defendant for his case.

Defendant

After being sworn in, Jones stated first that he had begun to live in the rental unit in mid August, and that Smith brought over a lease to him later—he couldn't remember the date. But he insisted that he occupied the property before he was required to sign the lease. He also said he remembered being told about the late penalty, but didn't realize how much extra money he would owe very quickly once missing his timely rental payment. The Court did not ask him if he could calculate 10% of his rent, but I had the distinct impression that he may have been mathematically challenged, unlike his mathematically astute adversary in court. He stated that after hearing just now in court that his late fees had run into the thousands of dollars, he wished he had realized in December how serious his debt would be, and he would have moved then. But he, as well as Mr. Smith, hoped that he would find a job and be able to catch up the rent quickly.

Jones further testified that he had made three payments of $300.00, not two as Smith said, always leaving them where he left rent payments in earlier months, at Mr. Smith's door. How did he make the payments? By money order. Did he have the stubs? No, the stubs were in a storage unit where he had put his belongings after being evicted, and he had defaulted on the storage rental as well, and had been locked out of his unit.

Mr. Jones was ready to rest his case, and he had not addressed the matters he brought up in his Answer about having tried to get a magistrate to interrupt the setting out of his belongings when he was evicted. The Court had already wondered about this contention prior to the hearing, and had looked on the county's court records to get the case number and details of the eviction. I had been unable to find the case anywhere.

The Court asked Mr. Jones to describe the eviction event, hoping that Jones would volunteer information about being served with the ejectment action. Already there was developing in the Judge's mind the possibility that Mr. Smith had circumvented the court in evicting Jones. But Mr. Jones had not brought any such records with him to court. So neither Smith nor Jones had any document showing that a legitimate eviction had actually been conducted by a court in February. Yet Jones had stated that he received notice of an eviction action in late January.

The Court's clerk, meanwhile, had been furiously searching the county's database for evidence of an eviction, and passed several notes indicating that she had been unable to find any record of such a case. I turned again to the Defendant and asked him whether or not he had been at home when the set out of his possessions took place. I wanted to know if he had seen a constable, seen a Writ of Ejectment, anything that would indicate that his eviction had taken place under the auspices of the court. No, he was not there at the time and a friend had called him to tell him that his belongings were being put out beside the road, and neighbors were picking over them as they spoke.

At this point, I had come to the conclusion that I would continue the case for a week and order both parties to return with various documents, including, as I specified, receipts and other documents relating to the eviction. Both parties made a note of the new court date and the gavel came down.

When the Court reconvened the following week, surprisingly each party had papers proving the eviction to have been properly filed, though it had been filed under landlord Smith's business, accounting for why a search under his name had not turned up the filing.

The extra week gave the Court the opportunity to mull over the case, however, and by the time the hearing reconvened, I had decided the case, subject to any additional evidence that might change the scenery. None did, and the Judgment followed.

THE JUDGMENT

1. The Court finds first that Mr. Jones defaulted on his rent for December and January and per his agreement with Smith repaid $600.00 of the $1,800.00 he owed for those two months. The Court further finds that Jones defaulted in February and that as of 17 February when he surrendered the property, he owed an additional $546.42 in rent proper, for a total of $1,746.42.
2. The Court weighed carefully the matter of late fees. A late fee against a residential tenant of 10% of outstanding rent *per day* strikes the court as offensive to the sensibility, especially since the late fees are not capped in any fashion and since the Plaintiff did not exercise his option to file for ejectment when the tenant first defaulted. The Court further noted at trial that the Plaintiff is a professor of computer science and is clearly well aware of how such late fees will mount up quickly, while the tenant appeared to have been less than fully aware of the magnitude of his mounting debt.
3. The Court understands that a late fee must be a stiff enough penalty to motivate a tenant to quickly cure default; however, a penalty that generates another entire month's rent in ten days constitutes, in the opinion of this Court, unjust enrichment on the part of the landlord.
4. The Court is reminded of the hypothetical question of whether a person would rather receive a million dollars in lump sum, or take payments for a month, one penny the first day, two additional pennies the second day, four additional pennies the third day, and so on, doubling the amount for a month of thirty-one days. Those who would take the lump sum would miss out. The payment on the thirty first day would be $10,737,418.24, and the total of all payments would be $16,106,127.36.
5. Mr. Smith's late fees did not promise to be quite so enriching,

but the Court did the math and discovered that as of January 6, this year, when late payments on a second month's rent would begin to be added, Mr. Jones already owed Mr. Smith $4,140.00, for a $900.00 per month rental unit. Even if Jones had repaid the base rent faithfully according to the secondary agreement—and had been able to pay February's rent on time, on the day he retired that base rent debt, he would have owed an additional $1,440.00 in late fees. Having defaulted on February's rent, Jones's running total was nearly twice as much.

6. Jones's situation was like a man bailing water out of a boat. During the first week, Jones was bailing out one gallon per day while more than two gallons were coming back in. During the second week, he was still bailing out a gallon per day while 1.4 gallons were coming back in. Even during the third week, which would retire a month's base rent, Jones was bailing out a gallon per day while a little less than a gallon was coming back in. But with the addition of another month's rent, the process started over again and just added to the running total. There was no way that the boat was not going to sink.

7. Added to that, Mr. Jones had become unemployed, which was the cause of his defaulting on December's rent in the first place. While not a defense against his owing the rent, his unemployment, fully known to Mr. Smith, certainly created circumstances under which Smith had reason to know that Jones would not be able to pay the rent plus high late fees that increased every day. Smith's decision not to file for ejectment promptly in December constitutes a failure to mitigate his damages, at the very least.

8. More fundamentally, however, the rate of the late fee is extraordinarily high for residential landlord-tenant leases, especially since it lacks any maximum amount of accrued penalty. Upon an assessment of the Plaintiff and the Defendant in their circumstances, the Court finds the late fee provision to be exploitative and is therefore unconscionable. It would be an affront to the integrity of the Court to enforce it, and I will not enforce it at all. The Court will instead enforce

the remainder of the contract, under which the Defendant is found to owe the accumulated rent and the unpaid utility bill, the total of which amounts is $2,456.26.

The Court renders Judgment for the Plaintiff and orders the Defendant to pay to the Plaintiff the amount of $2,536.26, which includes the court cost of $80.00.

Upon the Court's information and belief, the Defendant was unable to pay even this Judgment, and the Plaintiff recorded the Judgment and sought execution against the Defendant's only automobile, and was denied.

7
The Value of Tools

Most state laws provide various ways to acquire leverage over people who owe debts. Judgments in South Carolina Summary Courts can be recorded in the appropriate Circuit Courts, and domesticated in other states' courts, and those courts can take various measures to collect on judgments. Even at the Summary Court level, the Magistrate Court can issue a Distraint Warrant for Rent, to put some teeth into a prevailing landlord's demand to be paid what is owed. The distraint warrant in effect says, 'pay me or some of your stuff is mine.' The trouble comes when a landlord takes matters into his own hands. And when it involves a working man's tools, emotions run high. Here's a little case where weekend work ground to a halt because of a landlord's haste.

The Pleadings

Plaintiff Tom Smith complained to the Court that John J. Jones, acting for Jones, Inc., a property management company run by John and his wife Elizabeth, seized tools and other belongings of Plaintiff's at a residence then rented by Plaintiff Smith from Defendant, and that he refused to return them, causing damage to Smith for the loss of the use of the tools. Plaintiff asked for $7,500.00. Defendant Jones Answered that Plaintiff abandoned the rental property thereby justifying Defendant's taking possession of it and all possessions in it, and Jones counterclaimed that Smith owed him for his last month's rent and for damages to the rental property beyond normal wear and tear.

The Evidence

At trial, Smith was represented by Attorney Bill Williams. Williams had filed the complaint for Smith five days after the property had been seized by Jones. In his opening statement, Williams told the Court the case was a simple matter of unlawful seizure of property and loss of income as a result. In the action, filed as a Summons and Complaint, the Plaintiff asked the Court for the return of the property.

In anticipation of the trial, I surmised that the Plaintiff's filing was a mixture of strategy and mistake. Normally, a suit for possession of property would be filed as a Claim and Delivery, an action that can give rise to an order of dispossession—carrying the authority to enter with what force is necessary to take possession of wrongly detained property. However, the defendant filed a Summons and Complaint, which normally, in the Magistrate Court, does not encompass injunctions. But in his Complaint, Defendant requested that the Court award punitive damages and a judgment for the maximum jurisdictional amount of $7,500.00 in addition to an order for the return of the tools. A Claim and Delivery would not have allowed a request for a judgment other than for the simple value of the property detained (and any costs for the detainment), and then only if the property could not be had. Defendant's strategy seemed to be to use a Summons and Complaint in order to maximize the claim against the Defendant, possibly to promote settlement—which obviously had not happened.

The Court was certain that Smith was not the author of this strategy but that Attorney Williams was. In the Complaint, Defendant asked for a judgment of $7,500.00 for "punitive and active [sic] damages" and referred to Jones's action as not only seizure but "conversion to his own use." But what might eventually be shown to have been mistake was the failure to file two actions, one for claim and delivery and the other for the monetary judgment. It was not the first time, however, that the Court had had dealings with Attorney Williams, who had some eccentricities.

Plaintiff

Williams called Tom Smith as his only witness. In detailed and particular questions eliciting short and concise answers, Williams walked Smith through his case. Smith said that he had lived at 100 Short Street in a house rented from Jones for about seven and a half years. His common law wife, Mary Brown, left the residence nearly two years ago. She had been the only signer on the lease, and as Tom wished to continue living in the house, he and Jones had some discussions about what the terms would be. While Jones's dealings with Mary Brown at the point of her exodus seemed to the Court to be largely irrelevant, Smith did say that Jones had found some damage in the house that Smith agreed to repair and that Jones would return to Brown half of her security deposit. In consequence, Smith, who continued living in the residence, had no security money deposited with Jones.

Smith never signed a lease. Smith said that Jones talked about bringing a lease to him, but never did. Smith continued to rent month to month from Jones, and he paid his rent on time. Rent had been due the first of the month under Mary Brown's lease, and Smith himself actually paid it, giving it to Jones when Jones came by for it personally on the first, but never later than the fifth of the month, when the grace period expired.

Plaintiff Smith continued to live in the property for about a year and a half until August of the present year. Near the end of July, Jones and Smith agreed on the phone for Jones to collect rent at the rental property on August 1. Smith did not keep the appointment. Smith did not give a reason in his testimony, and Jones did not ask in his cross examination. In a follow-up phone conversation, Smith said he agreed to meet Jones there at the property on August 4 instead. But Smith said he was in a neighboring state doing a job on August 4 and that he was delayed overnight.

When he returned the next day, he said that the house had been broken into, the shed out back as well, and that all his tools had been taken. Four days later he filed suit. Smith said he called Jones and that Jones said he would return the tools if Smith paid August's rent. Smith refused, maintaining that Jones had not had any right to take the tools.

Attorney Williams never actually sought testimony from Smith about whether or not he had been moving, though Jones had stated in his Answer that he knew that Smith had actually signed a lease with someone else and had moved almost everything out of the residence. Williams simply asked Smith if he intended to leave the tools behind in the house permanently, and the answer to this mostly rhetorical question was predictably no.

Williams questioned Smith about the value of the tools and the work that he did with them, and how much work he had missed by not having his tools. Smith said the tools were worth $7,000.00 all together, that he did weekend jobs in houses—flooring, cabinets, painting and such—and that in the ten weeks Jones had been in possession of his tools, he could have made an average of $300.00 every weekend.

Jones had a few questions in cross examination, but seemed eager to begin making direct statements, especially at the prompting of his wife, whose coaching was quite audible, and who didn't seem to be able to keep from making statements herself. I assured her that if her husband called her as a witness, she would be able to testify later. She repeatedly apologized, but kept interrupting with questions or statements while her husband was making his faltering attempts at questioning Smith. Finally, she hid her face in her hands and tried to keep herself quiet.

Defendant

Plaintiff Smith rested and Jones took the stand. Jones introduced leases into evidence, the first lease with Mary Brown, when Jones was acting as a principal of Acme Properties, Inc., and a second lease with Brown under the name of Jones Properties, Inc. A third lease was between Jones Properties and Tom Smith, but was not signed. In all other respects, it was identical to the leases with Mary Brown.

Mr. Jones said that Smith had been a good tenant, always paying his rent on time. He referenced the departure of Mary Brown and wanted to give all the details about that incident, but by then the Court was convinced that the changing of the guard from Brown to Smith was irrelevant, and told Mr. Jones so. Jones continued, then, describing the events of the first of August of that year.

He agreed with Smith's testimony that the two had talked after August 1 and rescheduled their meeting for Jones to pick up the rent. Jones, however, said that when he went to the house on August 4, he found that the electricity had been turned off to the house, and peering in various windows, he could see that the furniture and other belongings appeared to have been removed from the dwelling.

Jones said he immediately called the Magistrate, which was this Court. He testified, as he had said in his Answer to the Complaint, that he wanted "to inquire about his legal rights to enter the rental home and take possession if possible." Defendant stated that "Judge Simms advised the Defendant that if the home was "abandoned," he could take immediate possession of the home and its contents."

The Court addressed Jones at this point, directing him not to draw the judge into his defense. I intended to address the matter of his claim of contacting the Court, when I issued a Judgment in the case, no matter whom I might find for.

Defendant Jones said that he determined that Smith had abandoned the property, and that he believed he had a right to take possession of the rental property. That same day, August 4, Jones called a locksmith (he entered the locksmith's invoice to prove damages of $111.00) and thus gained entry into both the house and a storage building on the property. Principally in the storage building or shed, Jones found a variety of tools. The tools included several ladders, a table saw, numerous heavy duty power cords, a generator, arc welding equipment and the like.

Jones took possession of the personal property, transporting it to another property of his. He moved into evidence numerous pictures of the tools, gathered together neatly in what the Court was told was Jones's garage. Some of the tools belonged to Smith and some to his son, as Smith had said in his testimony earlier. The property had remained in Jones's possession, and according to his sworn statement in court, at the time of the hearing it was still there and was not being used by Jones as his own or for his purposes.

Jones and his wife, Elizabeth, walked through the house on August 4 and noted various items and areas that they would subsequently address in repairs. Elizabeth took numerous pictures, copies of which Mr. Jones wanted entered as Defendant's exhibits. Hearing that Mrs. Jones had taken the pictures, the Court directed Mr. Jones to wait until she could take the stand to give foundational evidence. Jones continued, describing a few doors off their hinges, a missing doorknob, and several doors that had been outfitted with new, keyed door hardware. Jones was particularly focused on the doors. The original glass knobs had been replaced with keyed locks. Jones was adamant that these replacements throughout the little house were "damage."

He spoke about the numerous holes in the walls from picture hangers that needed patching before the interior could be repainted, which he said was required because the colors were strange. The outside also needed painting, and Jones wanted to recover the cost of that job. And Jones discovered the dishwasher needed repair of a broken hose. The Court asked Jones if he knew whether the dishwasher had been used during the previous seven and a half years. He said it was working when Smith and Mary Brown moved in, but that he knew that they didn't use it (how he knew, he didn't explain, but his admission that they didn't use it suggested that he would have to admit as well that Smith wasn't personally responsible for breaking it).

A day or so after August 4 of that year, Jones said he offered the return of Smith's personal property in exchange for Smith's payment of rent for August. Smith declined. Jones said the next communication he had with Smith was when he was served with Smith's suit for damages. Based on expenditures for repairs, Jones then counterclaimed for damages to the rental property and for August's rent of $750.00.

Williams for the Plaintiff cross examined at some length, asking Jones if he knew what collection of rent by distraint was—Jones did not. He asked why Jones broke into the property, which Jones denied, repeating that he used the services of a locksmith—Jones was making the usual assumption of persons not steeped in the language of the court, not realizing that "breaking" meant gaining unauthorized access, whether or not violent or destructive. Jones volunteered that he had decided to take possession because he "knew for a fact" that Smith was moving for good.

Williams then asked Jones if he knew what damage he saw in the house might have been caused during the tenancy of Mary Brown. Jones honestly said he didn't know. He couldn't be certain. He had almost never been in the house during those years Mary Brown was there.

After circling Jones several times with questions from various angles to get the same information, Williams sat down, and the Court dismissed the witness. I advised Mr. Jones at that point that it was now time for his wife to get a chance to testify, if he wanted her to. For all her previous urgency to interject, interrupt, advise, and otherwise get in a word edgewise, Elizabeth Jones said she didn't suppose she needed to add anything, but finally did whisper something to her husband and took the stand, just to talk about going through the house and taking the pictures. The photos were entered and the Court saw pictures of a few doors, door locks, and general need of sweeping. Jones also handed the Court a sheaf of receipts from "big box stores" for various hardware, paint and supplies. Elizabeth interjected that I should disregard two chocolate bars on one of the receipts. I studied the receipts briefly at the time and more fully later when I deliberated.

On cross, Williams asked one question only: did Elizabeth Jones know what damage she observed may have been caused by, or during the tenancy of, Mary Brown? Mrs. Jones also answered candidly that she couldn't be sure. She didn't know.

In brief summation, Williams repeated his opening speech, that the heart of the case was still that Jones had seized property without lawful cause or warrant, and that his possession of Smith's property had caused Smith monetary damage. For his closing, Jones did little other than to bring up the language of Landlord-

Tenant law, which he, or more likely his wife, had obviously researched, in the section that states that a lease signed by a landlord and delivered to a tenant but never signed, was considered to be in effect if the tenant then began making month to month payments. Williams was about to object, but Jones was finished almost as soon as he had started, and he abruptly ended his argument.

The Court then announced to the parties that it would take the matter under advisement and render a judgment within forty-eight hours. The trial had begun at 3:30, and it was just about 5:00 o'clock. I realized I would be weighing matters for much longer than anyone, least of all I, would be willing to wait in the courthouse. I carried the file home with me (not a habit of mine), and labored over it that evening. Minus the paragraphs that made findings of basic factual evidence described above, the Judgment follows:

THE JUDGMENT

First, as to the matter of the Defendant's basing his actions on what he calls the advice of this Court:

This Court is regularly contacted by landlords wanting to know the rights or constraints of landlord-tenant law. The answer provided by this Court, whether by the Judge or one of his staff, is never in the nature of attorney-type advice. A judge does not want to hear a party say, "The judge told me I had a good case." Yet, it is a legitimate function of the magistrate to help people know what the laws are and then to let them decide for themselves what kind of case to file.

In this case, the answer to the defendant's question was merely a summation of the rights and constraints provided under §27-40-730. The Court informed the caller of the definition of abandonment and the necessity of the landlord's valuation of personal property left in the rental unit at $500.00 or less.

South Carolina Law, §27-40-730, part of the Residential

Landlord Tenant Act, states in part that:

(a) The unexplained absence of a tenant from a dwelling unit for a period of fifteen days after default in the payment of rent must be construed as abandonment of the dwelling unit.

(b) If the tenant has voluntarily terminated the utilities and there is an unexplained absence of a tenant after default in payment of rent, abandonment is considered immediate and the fifteen day rule as described in (a) does not apply.
...

(d) When a dwelling unit has been abandoned or the rental agreement has come to an end and the tenant has removed a substantial portion of his property or voluntarily and permanently terminated his utilities and has left personal property in the dwelling unit or on the premises with a fair-market value of five hundred dollars or less, the landlord may enter the dwelling unit, using forcible entry if required, and dispose of the property.

(e) When a dwelling unit has been abandoned or the rental agreement has come to an end and the tenant has left personal property in the dwelling unit or on the premises in the cases not covered by subsection (d) above, the landlord may have the property removed only pursuant to the provisions of Sections 27-37-10 to 27-37-150. [These sections describe eviction procedures through the court.]

(f) Where property is disposed of by the landlord pursuant to subsection (d) and the property was in excess of five hundred dollars, the landlord is not liable unless the landlord was grossly negligent.

If the Landlord, the Defendant in this case, acted outside the boundaries of §27-40-730(e), it was not on the authority of this Court.

The Court addresses now the Plaintiff's Complaint,

focusing on the statutory definition of abandonment, the basis of Defendant's taking possession of the property rented to Smith. Upon the preponderance of the evidence as presented by both sides:

1. The tenant was not in default in rent when the landlord declared the property abandoned. The preponderance of the evidence shows that, while the Plaintiff had not paid his rent for August, which was due August 1, the grace period specified by law and observed between landlord and tenant had not expired when the landlord acted on August 4.

2. The tenant's absence from the residence was not an "unexplained absence" as referred to in §27-40-730. The intent of the phrase in the law is to identify not absence for an afternoon or even a weekend, but continued and substantial absence that, combined with default in rent and cancellation of utilities, reasonably suggest that a tenant has left permanently. The evidence in the record supports the Defendant's conclusion that Smith certainly was moving out for good, and Smith had not informed Jones that he was moving—he had in fact acquired another dwelling. However, whatever the tenant's intentions with respect to staying or moving out permanently, the landlord's determination of statutory abandonment on August 4 was unjustified by the facts known at that time. Jones's discovery of significant and valuable personal property in the shed belies his conclusion that Smith was already gone for good.

3. Jones valued the property at five hundred dollars or less for purposes of taking possession of the unit and Smith's personal property. Neither Jones nor Jones, Inc. filed for eviction against tenant Tom Smith, as would be required by §27-40-730(e) if a valuation were made of more than $500.00 in personal property value.

4. Jones was "grossly negligent," in the words of the statute, in his valuation of the property as worth no more than $500.00. At court, Jones testified during cross examination that the property "may have been" worth more than $500.00. The

evidence in fact shows that the property left at 100 Short Street was worth significantly more than that. The contents of the storage shed alone, as pictured in Defendant's own photographs, are clearly worth in excess of $500.00, as they include at least three ladders, a table saw, numerous heavy duty power cords, a generator, arc welding equipment, mechanic's tools and the like.

5. Defendant acted outside the constraints of the law in taking possession of the rental property on August 4 and in seizing Plaintiff's personal property beginning that day. His possession of that personal property now is entirely the result of his taking unlawful possession on August 4. Defendant's actions being premature, without proceeding under the auspices of §27-37-10 to §27-37-150, his possession of the property then and at the present time is unlawful.

6. Defendant, by taking and holding Plaintiff's property without distress warrant, without lawfully filing eviction, and having been grossly negligent in valuing the property, has damaged the Plaintiff by depriving him of the tools of his weekend work. While the Plaintiff testified that he *might* make $300.00 per job and *may* have missed ten job opportunities, the evidence is speculative. The Court cannot reasonably find that the Defendant's unlawful detention of the tools has cost the Plaintiff $3,000.00 in the past thirteen weeks, especially in a slow economy. No evidence was given of actual jobs offered to the Plaintiff that he had to decline. However, it is reasonable for the Court to conclude that the Plaintiff would have solicited job opportunities in that time, and would have performed one or two of them. The Court finds that the Defendant's possession of the Plaintiff's tools damaged the Plaintiff by $600.00. As a corollary, the Court finds that the value of the Plaintiff's tools in Defendant's possession is $7,000.00.

Turning to the Defendant's Counterclaim, the Court focuses on the Plaintiff's actions while he was a tenant, and in his act of leaving the property, and the Court continues with the following findings based on the preponderance of the evidence:

7. Tenant Smith did not give landlord Jones, Inc. proper notice of his ending the month to month tenancy as required by §27-40-770(b). Therefore, Smith owes rent for August of this year, in the amount of $750.00.

8. In the following particulars, Jones did not meet his burden in proving by the greater weight of the evidence that Smith had damaged the rental property beyond normal wear and tear: (a) Both John and Elizabeth Jones admitted that they did not know what, in the house, may have been damaged during the tenancy of lessee Mary Brown as opposed to that of Smith in the immediately previous year and a half, leaving open the question of whether Jones may have complaint against Brown; (b) The holes in the walls produced by picture hangers do not go beyond normal wear and tear; © Door knobs and locks changed by the tenant do not constitute damage; (d) The exterior of the house required repainting due to weather and not to any fault of the tenant; (e) The need of repainting the interior of the house is not beyond normal wear and tear unless the landlord can show abuse, and no evidence in the record supports such a conclusion; (f) The dishwasher cannot be said with any assurance to have been damaged during the exclusive tenancy of Smith.

9. Both Jones's testimony and the admission of Smith support a finding that Smith owes Jones the cost of re-hanging doors and the purchase and installation of missing door hardware. The evidence supports a finding that the cost of this work is $115.63.

10. Defendant-landlord's laches in the matter of his counterclaim, concerning keys and any related damages, bars his recovery on these matters.

On the basis of these factual findings, my Judgment is as follows:

The Plaintiff filed a Summons and Complaint, under the provisions of which the Magistrate Court does not regularly issue an order for the dispossession of property, since the law provides for such an order under title 22, article 13 (Claim and Delivery), a separate filing. However, the facts of this case lead to findings that invoke the provisions of §27-40-780(b) and §27-40-610(b), under which this Court may issue injunctive relief to the tenant.

The Court therefore issues and orders said injunctive relief for landlord's unlawful entry into the rental unit or for landlord's noncompliance with the rental agreement. The landlord's possession of the tenant-plaintiff's personal property was and is the direct result of the landlord's unlawful entry upon the rental property and taking possession thereof. The Court therefore orders the Defendant immediately to return to the Plaintiff his personal property, consisting of all those items described particularly at trial and being kept on landlord's property. The Defendant shall allow the Plaintiff access under the watch care of the Constable of this Court, at a time suitable to both parties and as soon as practicable.

In the alternative, should the personal property not be able to be had immediately, then upon the submission of Affidavit to that effect by Plaintiff, this Court shall issue an Amended Judgment for $7,000.00 against the Defendant, in addition to any other order encompassed in this present Judgment.

As to the Plaintiff's Complaint, in addition to the injunction as ordered above, the Court finds for the Plaintiff for $600.00, plus reasonable attorney fees of $300.00, as provided in §27-40-780(b), plus the cost of this action, which is $80.00.

As to the Defendant's Counterclaim, the Court finds for the Defendant and orders the Plaintiff to pay to the Defendant

$865.63.

The Counterclaim setting off the Complaint in part, the Court renders Judgment for the Plaintiff and orders the Defendant, in addition to complying with the injunctive order, to pay to the Plaintiff $114.37.

In the course of the hearing, I had sized up the Defendant and his wife as being a bit eccentric but of good character and principles, and I believed that while they would not like having to pay Smith anything, they would rather pay him $114.37 and give him his things back, than to pay him $7,000.00. I really didn't think they were the sort of folks who would abscond with the tools, which they had carefully kept, and then tell the Constable with an innocent shrug that somebody stole them the night after they got the Judgment. And they didn't. They cooperated fully.

And Smith, also fundamentally a man of good character, played his part to the end as he had always been—a good tenant. When he got his tools back, he declined the check for $114.37, offered his hand to Mr. Jones, and left on good terms.

Of course, he still had to pay his lawyer.

8
WHEN IS A DOWN PAYMENT
NOT A DOWN PAYMENT?

Most moderate size towns have numerous used car companies. Where there are car dealers, there are lawsuits, some justified, some not. Some of these companies' policies are designed to ensure that whenever they take money, they never refund it. Sometimes that's just, sometimes not. Here's a case where he said refund, she said not.

THE PLEADINGS

John Smith filed a Complaint against Jones Car Lot, a small operation dealing almost exclusively in vehicles purchased from one of several nearby auto auctions. Smith alleged that he had paid Bill Jones, the owner, $500.00 "toward the purchase of" a truck, which Jones would have to find for him. Smith claimed Jones never found the truck and then would not refund his $500.00.

In its Answer, Jones Car Lot admitted it could not find a truck of the specified kind in the price range Smith wanted, but that Smith applied the $500.00 toward another car, and when Smith failed to follow up by getting financing on his own, the deal fell through. Jones said its policy was that down payments are "not refundable, yet transferable."

THE EVIDENCE

Plaintiff

At trial, Smith said he was a merchant marine who was out in the Atlantic for a couple of months but staying in touch with his friend Mr. Adams. In one of their phone conversations, Smith said he needed a vehicle when he got home, and Adams, who had dealt successfully with Jones Car Lot before, recommended Jones.

While still at sea, Smith called Jones and told him he wanted either a Cadillac Escalade or a GMC Denali, in a range of several recent years. Jones said he would be glad to look for a truck, if Smith would send him a check for $500.00 as "good faith money" to show he was serious. Smith said he would get back to him in a day or so. Meanwhile, he talked with Adams again, who himself called Jones from stateside. Adams was shortly a witness for Smith and testified that Jones assured him that if he was not able to find a truck within the make and year range Smith wanted, "he will get his money back."

On the basis of this assurance, Smith called Jones again and confirmed the deal. He sent Jones the money. In about three months, Smith returned to the States and home, where he went to the Jones Car Lot. Jones was not there. His office manager Ms. Zieglar said he was at a car auction. She knew of the business Smith and Jones were doing, and assured Smith that Jones would find a truck for him.

Smith returned to the car lot the next day, and Jones again was not there. He made several trips with the same result, finally catching Jones at the lot. Jones told him he hadn't been able to find a truck for him. Disappointed, Smith said he would look elsewhere and asked for his money back. By this time, Ziegler was present for the conversation, and both Ziegler and Jones encouraged him to look around for something else on the lot. In fact, Smith said, he was in need of a car for his son, and he spotted an Acura that looked interesting. After test driving the car, he asked if he could transfer the $500.00 he had already paid Jones toward the purchase of the Acura. Zieglar and Jones happily said yes, and Zieglar began talking to Jones about financing.

Zieglar made out applications for financing and faxed them to one of the companies they dealt with. The application was rejected. Zieglar then faxed an application to another company, which also turned Mr. Smith down. Ms. Zieglar told Smith that he could go look for financing on his own and then come back when he had it and they would do the deal.

Smith left the car lot and returned in a few days saying that he had changed his mind and didn't want the car. He told them just to give his money back. That's when the dispute began. Zieglar pointed behind the counter in the office to a sign on the wall that said, "Down Payments are Not Refundable but Transferable." Smith countered that Mr. Jones himself had promised him he could get his money back. Smith and Zieglar went a round or two on the matter, and Smith finally left. He filed suit the next day.

Before concluding his testimony, Smith expressed irritation that Jones himself was not at the hearing. He had filed suit against the company, of course, but he thought Jones would be there. Instead, the business was represented at the hearing solely by Ms. Zieglar.

Defendant

Zieglar gave every appearance of having had some legal training. She had been employed by the business for some years and clearly had handled lawsuits before. As a non-lawyer, she acted for the company by statutory permission regarding magistrate courts. Her cross examination of Smith consisted entirely of leading questions, permissible on cross, posed in rapid fire manner and demanding a series of yes or no answers. She hoped to establish through the additional testimony that Smith was aware of the policy of no refunds, that he had initiated the request for his $500.00 to be transferred to a down payment on another vehicle, and that it was his fault the sale did not go through.

When Zieglar's cross examination was complete, Plaintiff Smith had no further direct testimony and rested his case. The Court half expected Zieglar to move for a directed verdict, but she didn't. The motion, if it had been made, would have been denied anyway, as the Court did not have enough evidence yet and had developed a few questions of its own for both parties.

In presenting the Defendant's case, Zieglar was adamant in her testimony that the company's policy was clearly posted and that Smith should have known he could transfer his down payment but not have it refunded. While she didn't dispute the major facts as Smith represented them, she did say that he had committed to buying the Acura but dropped the ball when he had to get financing. She emphasized the work that Jones Car Lot did for Mr. Smith in going to many auto auctions, and then in drawing up all the paperwork for the sale of the Acura.

Smith had a few, mostly irrelevant questions to ask Zieglar, to a few of which Zieglar objected, and the Court sustained. Smith then said with resignation that he didn't have any more questions.

The Court had a few of its own, however. I asked Ms. Zieglar first of all about her statement in the Answer (she had made out the pleading) that the policy of "non-refundable but transferable" "applies to everyone who chooses to give a deposit on a vehicle." She said yes. I asked if the policy were in writing anywhere other than the sign on the wall. No. I asked if she had spoken to Mr. Smith who was at sea when he made the deal with Bill Jones to find a truck. No. I asked if she had overheard the conversation, and the answer to that was also no.

Then I asked Zieglar to walk me through a typical car sale where Jones Car Lot did the financing. She gave about eight steps beginning with selection of the car and test driving, then including financing applications, and ending with a sit down with the customer. What, the Court asked, did that sit down entail. She said it was at this last step that Jones Car Lot laid out all the papers, had the customer sign the financing contracts and bill of sale, and write a check for the down payment (or pay cash). So, the Court asked, the down payment is made in the last step? Yes.

Recalling the matter of both Smith's and Adams's phone calls to Jones, the Court asked both those witnesses to repeat their testimony of exactly what Jones had said. Smith reaffirmed that Jones said, verbatim, to send him $500.00 in "good faith money, to prove you're serious" about buying a car. Adams reaffirmed for his part that Jones had said, "he'll get his money back" if a satisfactory truck could not be found. Finally, the Court asked if Smith had ever heard anything from Mr. Jones about a policy of not refunding money. Smith strongly said no.

THE JUDGMENT

As read in court, I rendered this Judgment in the case:

> The issue before the court is whether or not Defendant Jones Car Lot has a right to retain $500.00 paid to them by Plaintiff John Smith.
>
> Plaintiff claims the $500.00 was good faith money for Bill Jones as agent for Defendant to look for a truck for him, which Jones did not succeed in finding. Defendant claims that its policy is no refunds on down payments on vehicles, that Plaintiff was informed of this when he came to Jones Car Lot, that he transferred the $500.00 he paid for a fruitless search to the purchase of an Acura, and that because of Jones's work on the application toward Smith's purchasing the Acura, Jones has a right to keep the $500.00 as a down payment on that vehicle.
>
> On the preponderance of the testimony the Court finds the following to be facts:

1. John Smith and Bill Jones agreed that Jones would look for a truck for Smith for $500.00 in good faith money. No evidence exists that Mr. Smith had any form of notice of Jones Car Lot's policy of non-refundable payments. In fact, Jones assured Smith by way of witness Adams that he would get his money back if the search for the truck were unsuccessful.

2. Upon his return stateside, Smith visited Jones Car Lot several times and after determining that the truck would not be found as specified by make, year, and price, he did initiate conversations about transferring the $500.00 to the purchase of an Acura for his son.

3. In Jones Car Lot's process, a down payment is not made or processed on a vehicle until all finance applications have been made, submitted and approved, and the customer sits down with an agent of the business to finalize the deal. Sale of the Acura never reached that point. When Smith finally demanded his money back, his $500.00 check had not been officially transferred as a down payment on any particular car.

4. Consequently, Mr. Smith did not put $500.00 down on a vehicle. An agreement was reached between the parties as to what the $500.00 was for. In that sense, there was a contract, and Jones did not perform on that contract. Even if there had not been a contract, the Court would treat the $500.00 as subject to the principles of equity. Jones Car Lot did not provide a service to Mr. Smith constituting *quantum meruit* for $500.00. It would be unjust enrichment for them to retain Mr. Smith's good faith money.

Judgment is for the Plaintiff for $580.00, which includes the court cost of $80.00.

Jones Car Lot was in court the next day defending itself against another, unrelated suit, and Jones prevailed. You win some, you lose some.

9
ZERO POWER BILLS

Out of a hundred eviction filings in my court, perhaps five will go to trial. The five that eventuate in hearings usually involve interesting stories, although some renters will ask for a court date simply to extend the time they have to move. Statistically, about seventy-five percent of the time that ejectment actions wind up in court, the plaintiff/landlord prevails. But statistics do not influence the Court in deciding the next case to come along. It's always the evidence.

THE PLEADINGS

In this interesting landlord-tenant case, Sharon Smith rented an apartment to Jerry Jones in November of a given year, and as part of the lease agreement, Jones would put the apartment's electric bill in his own name. There is nothing unusual there, or in the fact that Smith came later to the court to apply for a Rule to Show Cause for the ejectment of Jones, claiming that Jones had not put the electric bill in his name, as agreed. In filing the action, Smith, who did a lot of evictions through the court, checked "Failure to pay rent" as her reason, and alluded cryptically to other problems in a "catch all" sort of note that she added to every ejectment application she made.

Jones was served with the Rule to Show Cause by the constable and came to the court the same day. He strongly denied that the suit was about rent, and stated that he had paid his rent. A check of the court-prepared copy of the Rule revealed that the court clerk had checked "failure to pay rent" but had not added the "catch all" phrase alluding to lease violations. The clerk did some checking with Plaintiff Smith as well as consulting the original ejectment application. She discovered that Smith did not mean to check "rent" because she admitted that Jones had, indeed, paid his rent.

Her grounds for this ejectment were the lease violations. The clerk reprinted the Notice correctly and Jones was served. Jones asked for a hearing on the basis of a general denial.

THE EVIDENCE

Plaintiff
At trial, Smith testified briefly to the key facts as she saw them. In November, Jones had signed a lease agreement, placed in evidence, agreeing to put the electric bill in his name. In March of the following year, Smith received information from her company's home office in another state that the bills had been coming to them, and that the home office had paid them. Smith then wrote a letter to Jones, included copies of the bills, and demanded repayment for them, as well as notifying Jones that he had not complied with the lease and demanding that he do so. Smith rested her testimony with the statement that Jones had not repaid her for the power bills her company had paid from November through May.

Jones, *pro se,* declined to cross examine, preferring just to lay out his case.

Defendant
Jones gave a fuller account. He testified that after signing the lease he had proceeded to contact the power company and request a transfer of his account from his previous address to his new address in Smith's apartment building. He made a payment of $200.00 to the power company as a transfer fee. For some reason, the power bill for November came to Smith at the company office, and it was for $34.14, for a partial month. Tenant Jones said that sounded right, and he paid Smith for it. Jones's bill for December, however—which came to him at the rental unit—, showed "$0.00" was due. He didn't understand. When January's bill came showing the same amount—nothing owed—Jones went to Smith's office to ask what the problem was.

Jones testified that Smith told him his power bill was between him and the power company, and that she couldn't explain the zero bills. Jones came back again to Smith in February when yet another bill for nothing came in the mail. Smith still had no answers.

Jones did not pursue the problem to solve it, however (as the Court noticed) but let the matter continue through most of April before calling the power company again, at which time he was told he needed to pay a $200.00 transfer fee. While he argued that he had already done so, he paid the fee. May's statement showed the power account had been transferred. Smith's home company's payments for Jones's electric bills had ended with April, and the company informed Smith in May of the total Jones owed them, which according to Smith was $969.00. The power company also scheduled a cutoff, which they performed when May's bill went unpaid.

Jones offered no proof of his having paid the first $200.00 fee in November, but the Court found the testimony credible nonetheless. Jones exhibited a strange willingness to allow a situation to continue that could not help but end up in trouble, but the Court noted that Jones was a very young man, about twenty-five, and that his two apartment-mates were around his age. They also were lacking in maturity and experience, and may not have realized what difficulties were brewing.

The Court posed a few questions to Jones while he was on the stand. Did he believe that someone else was paying his electric bill for him? Did he not anticipate that at some point he would have to pay the total that was accumulating somewhere? Did he not hold out some money from his regular income to pay the bill when things finally got straightened out? And why had he not paid Smith's bill for $969.00 when presented with it in May?

Jones indirectly implied that he didn't have the money to pay the power bill, that it had been spent on other things, month by month, as he got the zero bills. But more directly, he said he didn't pay the $969.00 bill because he disagreed with it. He couldn't see, from the copies of bills given him in May, where Smith had come up with $969.00. He challenged the Court to explain it as well.

The Court asked Smith to explain to the Court and to Jones where she got her figures, and Smith approached the bench, used a calculator, added figures in the same box from each bill, and arrived at $969.00. The figure included late fees for each month the bill had not been paid. It appeared to the Court at that point that Smith's home office had not satisfied the bill in a timely fashion itself, for reasons unknown—perhaps merely because they wondered why they were getting it.

Smith cross examined, asking Jones questions that verified the simple testimony Smith had offered earlier. The Court basically had the statements of the two parties with no other witnesses and virtually no testimony elicited as a part of cross examination.

The facts seemed clear to the Court, however, and as I retired to deliberate, I put two and two together, and came up with a very firm four.

THE JUDGMENT

The preponderance of evidence in this case leads the Court to make the following findings of fact:

1. The evidence supports a finding first that tenant Jones made a good faith attempt to transfer the electricity account from his previous residence to his new apartment, paying the required amount for the transfer. Subsequent bills Jones received for $0.00 confused him, but he did not realize that the account may not have been transferred properly. There was no testimony from either party to enable the Court to know why Jones's power bills were now going to Smith's home office. [While outside court, and directed to the court clerk, landlord Smith had speculated that Jones had made use of information he should not have had, to have his power bill sent to Smith's home office, nothing was said on this subject in court.] There is not any evidence to suggest that Jones had any knowledge of the exact amounts of bills that accrued thereafter, since he did not see them. The Court cannot think of any reason that Jones

would have attempted to transfer his bill to the home office of Smith's apartments, when his tenancy relied on his conforming to his lease. Granted, some tenants jeopardize their continued tenancy by violating terms of their lease or by nonpayment of rent, but the particular details of this case convince me that Jones was not engaged in a scheme to evade his monthly power bills.

2. It is further the finding of this Court that Landlord Smith did notify the tenant-defendant on May 24 of this year of the accrual of power bills, then being received by the home office, and that these bills were due and owing to Smith's company, which as of this date has satisfied the bills with the electric company. The Court also finds, and it is not contested in the testimony, that the tenants did not pay the amount due and demanded in May. Smith filed suit for possession of the apartment on June 16, and an amended application was filed and served on June 22.

3. Plaintiff's evidence states that the tenants did not transfer their account until March 12 of this year. The Court believes that this date does not reflect the date on which the tenants made their good faith effort to—and completed the steps, including payment of a transfer fee of $200 to—transfer the account. Although there is not sufficient evidence to make a finding of fact, it appears likely that the power company made an error in processing the first transfer request, an error that resulted in the Plaintiff's home office getting the bills for the actual power usage, and in the Defendant's getting a copy of the same bill, but for $0.00.

4. Because the Court finds that Jones made a good faith effort to comply with his lease in transferring the power bill and believed he had done so, the Court is not willing to find that the tenant failed to comply with the terms of his lease upon renting the unit on November 3 of last year.

5. However, the Court will not be complicit in enabling Jones to experience a windfall by way of escaping utility payments for the period of December through the recent cutoff. The

preponderance of testimony and documentary evidence shows the Court that Jones owes $951.00, which is the total of new utility charges since the last bill Jones paid, for part of November, until the date of cutoff, minus the late charges, which, because Jones did not get his bills, he should not be responsible for paying.

6. The amount Jones owed from December through the spring was unknown to him. Even after Smith became aware of the bills and informed Jones of the amount he owed, Jones disputed the amount owed. It was therefore necessary that this Court make a determination of the amount owed as the result of a hearing, which hearing we have just concluded. Therefore, the exact amount owed has only now been determined, and the Court gives notice to Jones today that this amount is owed in order to come into compliance with his lease.

7. Again, the Court finds that the amount owed by Jones to come into compliance with the lease is $951.00. Since the terms of South Carolina's Landlord-Tenant Act, § 27-40-610, provide that a tenant be given fourteen days to come into compliance with the lease in a matter not affecting health or safety, the Court therefore orders that the tenants pay the landlord this amount by close of business on Friday, July 16 of this year. In the event of nonpayment of this amount, the tenant will be in violation of the lease, and will be ejected.

The Court then continued the hearing until Tuesday, July 19, at 9:00 a.m., informing the litigants that if, at that time, Jones was not in compliance, then upon Smith's affidavit, her Application for Ejectment would be approved automatically without need of further hearing, and Smith could apply for a Writ of Ejectment immediately.

When Smith first filed her eviction action, she had also filed a Summons and Complaint for the amount of the power bills. As part of the Court's Judgment, I added that should the amount

Jones owed not be paid, any subsequent action in Summons and Complaint filed by the landlord could go forward with the findings of the eviction hearing admissible as fact.

Jones paid the bill.

10

CAPULET AND MONTAGUE, SORT OF

One of the more difficult civil issues to come before a magistrate is a Restraining Order. Some of these actions are heartbreaking because they often involve the disintegrating relationships of people who should be close friends or who are even family members. Except in emergencies when the Family Court is not in session, a magistrate in S. C. will not normally handle an Order of Protection, an action for a Restraining Order against a spouse. But other family members can square off against each other in Magistrate Court at any time, and I have had spells when it seemed that every day someone filed for an Restraining Order over the most irrational and unprovoked behavior. And people who were once married but no longer, or who were lovers but no more, occasionally become embroiled in a bitter aftermath, and find their way to my courtroom.

Every once in a while an interesting twist will take place on the former lover story. Here's a case where the lovers were not former at all.

THE PLEADINGS

Plaintiff Juanita Smith filed a Complaint and Motion for Restraining Order on behalf of her daughter Alejandra, a fifteen-year-old minor, against Amanda Jones, age nineteen. In South Carolina, a magistrate level Restraining Order is based on a finding of harassment or stalking, any degree. The Complaint form asks for three incidents supporting this claim. Mrs. Smith listed three incidents alleging sexual activity between her daughter and the Defendant Amanda Jones. No Answer is needed from a Defendant in a restraining order action. The Defendant either appears for the hearing stated on the Summons or Temporary Restraining Order he/she is served with, or she doesn't, and in the latter case, almost certainly the Restraining Order would be granted. Nevertheless, the Defendant Ms. Jones called the court and said she would definitely come to the hearing.

THE EVIDENCE

When the parties assembled, both Juanita Smith and her husband Carlos were there with their daughter Alejandra. Juanita and Carlos were a worried looking pair, but the body language between them and their daughter did not suggest, interestingly enough, a high level of hostility or alienation between parents and child. In fact, during the entire proceeding, Alejandra did not appear to be overly rebellious against her parents. Amanda Jones's parents were also with her though not from any legal need, since Amanda was no longer a minor and had been named in the suit alone. The Joneses appeared markedly more confident than the Smiths and were clearly there mainly for support, though the mother eventually testified.

Alejandra Smith was a compact girl with midnight hair and deep brown eyes, which she was dobbing with a tissue before things even got started. Amanda Jones was a tall and slender brunette with short hair and a Winona Ryder look about her. She did not appear to be nervous, but neither was she cocky, which, in my experience, Defendants in restraining order actions often are. The two girls cast occasional, brief looks across the aisle at each other not accompanied by any discernable messages.

I began with an off the cuff version of my usual speech before restraining order hearings, which was designed to put people at relative ease and to clarify for the defendant, in particular, what a Restraining Order is and is not. I explained that a Restraining Order is a civil action that functions as something of a bridge between civil and criminal actions. If granted, it is a civil order based on a finding of criminal conduct, namely harassment or stalking. Since it is civil in nature, however, it does not result in either creating a criminal record or adding to one. Hearing such information, I have seen many defendants appear visibly relieved.

However, when I continue by saying, *"unless* the defendant disobeys the court order, and then the matter becomes criminal," the relief sometimes fades and the nervousness sets in again.

With preliminaries taken care of, the parties testified.

Plaintiff

Plaintiff Juanita Smith began testimony by stating that her daughter Alejandra and Amanda Jones had become friends more than a year ago when Amanda was a senior in high school and Alejandra was a freshman at the same school. Alejandra was now a sophomore, and Amanda had graduated. Mrs. Smith said the girls were close during the previous summer, before Alejandra's sophomore year began, and that she wondered but did not know that the two may have been attracted to each other in something more than friendship.

Her notion became knowledge when on September 15, Amanda was visiting at the Smith's house, and Juanita Smith looked through the window of her daughter's bedroom and saw Amanda on top of Alejandra in the bed. Both girls were partly undressed. Smith went inside, opened Alejandra's door and told Amanda to leave. Amanda left. Smith said she had a short talk with Alejandra. She didn't testify as to what Alejandra said, but Smith was extremely uneasy about describing the encounter and left the impression that she was neither explicit nor particularly firm with her daughter.

A couple of months went by and Smith was not aware of any further contact. However, on November 14, around 3:00 a.m., Smith heard what she believed was Alejandra and Amanda having sex in Alejandra's bedroom. She didn't say, but she left the Court with the impression that she was awakened by the sounds. She went to the bedroom, opened the door and found what she feared, Alejandra and Amanda in total undress, having sex. Both girls quickly covered up. Smith said she told Amanda she had five minutes to get out of the house or she was going to call the police. Amanda left.

Smith again attempted to talk with Alejandra, and Alejandra

said, "I'm drunk." Smith believed that Amanda Jones had provided the alcohol. Smith found a liquor bottle in the bedroom and disposed of it. Though she had no evidence of it, she also believed that Alejandra was under the influence of some other drug, perhaps marijuana.

It was January before Smith had another run in with Amanda. On January 5 of the present year at about 9 p.m., Mrs. Smith again caught Amanda in Alejandra's bedroom and again gave her five minutes to get out. The Court asked why five minutes. Well, Smith said, the girls were again in bed and totally undressed, and she gave Amanda the five minutes to get her clothes on. The Court asked Smith if she had not seen Amanda come into the house. Smith appeared flustered to have failed to give me the information earlier that on these two occasions just described, when she caught Amanda in the house, Amanda had gained access through Alejandra's bedroom window. Alejandra had removed the screen, and Amanda had put a barrel on the ground below the low window and crawled in.

It was after the January incident that Juanita Smith made a police report. She wanted the matter investigated as a sex crime of some sort. She had not subpoenaed a police officer for the hearing, and so the police report she had included with her Complaint and Motion to open this case did not come in as evidence. I knew from the pleadings that the report had been filed, sent up to the Sex Crimes team for further investigation, and that apparently nothing more had been done with it.

Things quieted down after January, until March 5 of this year when Juanita Smith found out that her daughter had not been at school that day, and upon investigation, including grilling Alejandra, she learned that Amanda had picked her up that morning from the bus stop and the two had been together all day. Smith seemed uneasy at this point and appeared to be considering whether or not to reveal any more details about what she may have known of the girls' activities that day. Smith told her daughter she didn't want her spending time with Amanda Jones.

Then on March 17, Juanita Smith said she found her daughter's cell phone and looked on it. She didn't explicitly say that she was searching Alejandra's room but in fumbling for exact words she implied that she was. She looked through Alejandra's messages and found several from Amanda, and to Amanda, that were laced with sexual and romantic references. One of the messages from Amanda was a picture message, and she said the picture was one that Amanda had taken of herself nude. The text spoke of Amanda's wanting Alejandra badly, and describing various other things in detail that made Smith blush while she was testifying. At the Plaintiff's side, Alejandra's elbows were on the table, her head in her hands. On the other side of the aisle Amanda blanched slightly, but seemed otherwise unashamed.

Finally, Smith said she returned home from work mid day in early June and found Amanda and Alejandra "having some sexual conduct." That's when she came and filed for a Restraining Order.

Smith was finished with her testimony and asked her husband if he had anything to add. I directed her to wait to see if the Defendant had any questions to ask. Amanda's parents immediately asked if they could ask some questions. Technically, since Amanda was of age, and Amanda alone was the Defendant, I told them I shouldn't allow them to act essentially as her lawyers. But this proceeding, like many others of this sort, invited a kind of informality that might help to settle things if it didn't conversely cause them to degenerate into open argument. The Joneses were already offering some explanation, the Smiths were responding, and the self confident Amanda appeared finally to be becoming overwhelmed with grief about what she believed she saw coming. The Joneses said they knew that several times the Smiths had told Amanda not to contact Alejandra again, and that they believed Amanda had broken things off, but that it was Alejandra who called Amanda again or begged her to come over.

It was clear from just a few seconds of this sort of breakdown in the strict order of the courtroom that neither set of parents wanted the girls to be pursuing a same-gender relationship. None of the parents would articulate this specific objection at this moment, almost certainly because they were unwilling to voice a difference with the prevailing gender politics of the age. But this was most certainly their problem with the pair. It had nothing to do with one set of parents not liking the daughter of the other parents, but rather with a preference for their daughters to have heterosexual romances. In fact, I had the distinct impression that if one or the other had been a boy, they would have been mutually happy for their children to be in love and be happy. At the same time, I felt certain that they would have been vastly more alarmed if either of their girls had been having sex with a *boy*. The same gender activity probably seemed to them to be more like youthful experimentation, while opposite gender sex would have been undeniably more serious.

Presently, I got everyone quiet and back on the same page—mine—and had Amanda ask any questions she wanted to. She seemed more timid than I thought she might, but she did ask Juanita Smith if it were not true that Alejandra was just as responsible in the two being together as she was. Smith had to admit that as far as she knew, that was true, but that wasn't the point. She was Alejandra's mother. Amanda asked if it weren't also true that Alejandra had texted her just as much as she had Alejandra—same sort of question, and the answer was the same, except that Smith added she didn't know if Alejandra had taken pictures of herself naked to send to Amanda. Amanda didn't volunteer the information and didn't have anything more to ask.

Carlos Smith then testified briefly to pretty much the same things, further explaining what conversations he and his wife had had with the Defendant's parents. Mr. Smith now frankly said that he didn't think the relationship between his daughter and Amanda was appropriate. He didn't elaborate. The Joneses had no questions of Carlos, and he stepped down.

I asked if there were anything more from the Plaintiffs, and Alejandra, whose parents had not called her to give any testimony—no doubt because they knew she didn't want them or anyone else to keep Amanda away from her—raised her hand and asked, quivering, "Does it matter if I don't want her to stay away?" I couldn't have kept her from speaking before she did, and while I didn't allow her to continue if her parents' did not ask for her testimony—and they didn't—still I gathered all the confirmation I needed of her feelings on the subject. Alejandra was a little girl in love, or at least what passes for it at fifteen.

Defendant

When I asked Amanda if she wanted to present a defense to the Smith's request for a Restraining Order, she first froze, seemed uncertain, and then a look of defeat and resignation came across her face and she said in a little lost girl voice, "No," and seemed to shrink in her seat.

Some conversation went on at her table, and Amanda changed her mind and said she wanted her mother to testify. I swore in Mrs. Jones and she made a few statements reflecting the previous informal statements she made during the hubbub I allowed to go on during Defendant's cross examination. She characterized Amanda as a good girl and said she and Mr. Jones had expressed their concern to Amanda about the Smith's disapproval of the girls' relationship but she said she knew that Alejandra had done as much to encourage the relationship as Amanda had.

I knew that Mrs. Jones's and Amanda's protestations that Alejandra was just as aggressive in the relationship were basically irrelevant, since even if it were established that Alejandra welcomed Amanda's advances, it was not Alejandra's objection that mattered here, but that of her parents. I allowed Mrs. Jones to continue, however, not only to get the fullest picture of what was going on between all the players, but simply to give them all the opportunity to have their say. No one could say she didn't get to tell her story.

The Smiths had no questions for Mrs. Jones, and she took her seat. I ascertained that everybody was finished.

I needed to deliberate. Normally, in a Restraining Order, I would simply grant or deny it and then add my usual post-order speech. In this case, more words were called for, and I had to think things over. I announced a brief recess and went back to chambers to study over the matter.

One thing I was curious about as I thought about the context of the hearing was whether the Smiths' testimony was so well prepared that as a result it had been shorn of any indication of outrage, firmness, or explicit parental discipline they might have expressed with their daughter. The only other explanation was that Juanita Smith and her husband Carlos were ineffectual or overly permissive parents who simply did not know how to deal with their teenager and were hoping the Court would do it for them. Nevertheless, there was a genuine issue here for the Court. The parents had a right to object to the sexual conduct of another person, of whatever age or gender, toward their minor daughter.

First of all, a parent has a right to determine what kind of contact he or she wants her minor child to have. The Smiths had the right to say that the Jones girl's attentions were unwelcome, even if Alejandra herself wanted Amanda's attention, which, as it had become apparent to the Court, she did. Even so, to grant the motion for the Restraining Order, the Court would have to find that Amanda's attentions and advances toward Alejandra constituted harassment under the law. The relevant code section states:

> Harassment in the second degree means a pattern of intentional, substantial, and unreasonable intrusion into the private life of a targeted person that serves no legitimate purpose and causes the person and would cause a reasonable person in his position to suffer mental or emotional distress. Harassment in the second degree may include, but is not limited to, verbal, written, or electronic contact that is initiated, maintained, or repeated. §16-3-1700(B)

In the case of a parent filing for a minor child, the parent, not the child, gets to complain of "intrusion" and to claim "mental or emotional distress." But what of the Defendant's having "no legitimate purpose"? It was clear to me in this case that the legitimacy of the purpose had to be decided on the basis of whether or not the conduct itself were lawful, not on whether or not the targeted person, Alejandra, objected to it.

In this case, the law that came into play was §16-3-655, Criminal Sexual Conduct with a Minor. This particular section of S.C. law is lengthy and detailed, but essentially what it boiled down to for this case was that it is unlawful for a person over eighteen to have sex with a person of age fifteen even when the sex is consensual—in part because the fifteen year old is not considered to be able to lawfully consent to sex. Since these particulars fit the situation, the conduct was illegal, and by definition then, it could by no means be considered legitimate.

Consequently, whether or not the parents were being spineless about parenting, their Restraining Order was an appropriate legal action to take. Rather than go back in and sound overly technical, I returned with a more genial and softly delivered decision.

THE JUDGMENT

Usually when a Restraining Order is before me, it is between two people who can't stand each other. In fact, often both parties are harassing each other and I can't really say who started it or who is doing it worse. What we have here, however, is two girls who have amorous feelings for each other and they both want to have the contact they have, including sex.

The problem, young ladies, is that your parents don't want you to be involved with each other, and at this point in your lives, particularly for Miss Smith, your parents have a controlling interest. It is they who filed for the Restraining Order as your guardian, even though you didn't want them to. Even so, if they had complained about the attention Amanda was paying Alejandra but there had been nothing more than routine friendship, this Court would have dismissed the action. Under normal circumstances, this Court will not do the parents' job for them. What makes this complaint the business of the Court is the sexual element.

I know that the two of you have agreed several times to have sex—what the law calls "consensual,"—that nobody was forcing anybody. But you may not know that South Carolina law forbids a person of nineteen and a person of fifteen to have sex, even if consensual. The person of fifteen cannot legally consent to having sex with a person over eighteen.

For that reason, I must grant the Smiths' the Restraining Order they have asked for.

At this point, Amanda, who had seen it coming, didn't react more than a little, but Alejandra wailed softly and began crying, hands over her face. Turning to Amanda, I addressed her alone.

Miss Jones, I remind you now as I said at the top of this hearing, that this is a civil court order. It simply means that you are to have no contact with Alejandra for one year from today. That includes texting, email, phone calls, visits, or any indirect form of trying to get a message through to her. If you abide by this order, in one year it will go away. Only if you violate it will it become more serious. I want you to understand that the Smiths can call the police if you contact Alejandra, and you could be arrested. I know you don't want that. Do you understand?

Amanda nodded slowly and with great emotion. I asked if there were any questions. Little Alejandra worked her hand up in stages and then asked, "Does it make any difference if I turn sixteen during the year?" Quite honestly, I didn't know from a technical, legal standpoint whether or not her turning sixteen would have any compelling impact on the order, but I couldn't afford to waver, and I wasn't willing to modify the order at that point, so I said no, it wouldn't make a difference.

I then asked the Smiths to leave the courtroom first and instructed the Joneses to remain for a moment. I then gently brought the gavel down and dismissed the hearing. As the Smiths were leaving the back of the courtroom, I also rose to go, and glanced with some compassion on the wispy, confused nineteen year old Amanda, who finally had broken down and was sobbing profusely, as if her life were over.

About six months later our court clerk fielded a call from the Smiths asking what they could do if Amanda violated the order—apparently she had. But while they were told their only remedy at this point was to have Amanda arrested, they never did. I suspect they simply gave up and concluded that like it or not, the two were in love and would not be denied.

11

Fancy Footwork Attorney

The most interesting thing about some cases is not the issues involved but the performance of the lawyers. Indeed, some of the more routine cases become entertaining for nothing having to do with the actual facts involved, but because of the extraneous testimony invited by attorneys, much of it prompted by their colorful and evocative questioning.

Mind you, I have high respect for attorneys. I come from a family of ministers and lawyers and I have admiration for both. But I am not referring to misconduct of any sort, or even inexplicable or troubling eccentricities. The courtroom performance I'm referring to is the purposeful theatrics some attorneys display in order to set the scene for their cases or create sympathy for their clients.

I have sometimes insisted on cutting to the chase and reining in wandering lawyers, but often I just give them a long leash to run on. Without meaning to boast, usually I do see where they're going and usually it is toward what eventually will be shown to be relevant information. Occasionally, however, it is clear to me that an attorney is pursuing testimony that is not strictly relevant, not even generally relevant, but is designed to misdirect the judge—me. On such occasions, while I might not allow a *pro se* party to wander, I will generally allow an attorney to continue. I figure he may be turning his long leash into enough rope to hang himself (figuratively) with, or at the very least, to entertain us all.

Magicians have always employed misdirection to maximize the effectiveness of their illusions. They draw one's attention to their left hand while performing slight of hand with their right. Boxers do the same, feinting with one fist and then punching with the other. Muhmamad Ali was famous for his fancy footwork—"float like a butterfly"—back and forth all around the other pugilist, who then did not see the punch coming at lightning speed—"sting like a bee."

In this otherwise blasé eviction case. the thing to watch was the attorney, even though I knew that it was all smoke and mirrors.

THE PLEADINGS

Only about two months after renting the house at 100 Country Lane to Lana Jones, Dan Smith filed an Application for Ejectment against her for lease violations. Landlord Smith alleged that she installed a fence and had dogs inside it, had trashed piled up in both the front and back yards, had a junk car on the property, and put signs out front saying "Dogs for Sale"—all in violation of the lease. Tenant Jones filed a timely Answer saying that she had a witness who would corroborate Smith's statement that she could have dogs and a kennel out back. She said the trash was the temporary result of unpacking and that she needed time to clean it all up. She threw in a common statement made by defendants, that she was "disabled" (they rarely say how or offer medical proof). The case went to court.

PRETRIAL

Jones filed her Answer *pro se,* but as of the day of the hearing she had obtained counsel. That same day, in fact, the Court received, just prior to the hour of the hearing, an Answer and Counterclaim, with Jury Trial Demanded. over the signature of Attorney Travis Johnson.

When the hearing convened, the Court asked Johnson if he had pretrial motions to make, knowing that he did. Johnson approached and moved for a Jury Trial. I responded:

"Thank you, Mr. Johnson. Rule 13 of the Rules of Magistrate Court provides for a party's right to be heard before a jury if the request is made in writing at least five working days prior to the original date set for trial. Since the request is being made the day of trial, it is not timely, and respectfully, the request is denied. Anything else?"

Johnson said, "Your honor, may I see that rule?" Not seeing how feigning a lack of acquaintance with that rule would help his cause at all, I concluded rather quickly that Mr. Johnson really didn't know he was too late to ask for a jury. I opened my personal bench notebook to the appropriate page and rule and placed it on the front of the bench for him to inspect. He studied it a moment and then thanked me quietly and stepped back.

"Your honor," he continued, "this case is about some complaints Mr. Smith has about the visual appearance of the property [apparently, Johnson thought that there was some other kind of appearance than the "visual" kind], and about some dogs. And I think that if we can just have a few moments with Mr. Smith we might be able to come to some settlement whereby Mrs. Jones agrees to take care of most of these complaints within a certain number of days."

Taking seriously the general way in which the Magistrate Court in South Carolina is interested in promoting settlement, I directed them to a conference room outside the courtroom, then I went back to chambers while Smith and Jones tried to resolve the matter. But within five minutes, the clerk called me back.

Johnson said, "Well, your honor, we can't come to an agreement about the dogs, so I guess we'll proceed. But, your honor, I have just been retained by my client, and since we cannot have a jury trial, I would like to request of your honor a continuance to prepare for a hearing before your honor."

My honor usually grants continuances for parties whose lawyers are so lately obtained that they haven't had time to get a handle on the case; I figure it prevents a lot of appeals later. So I granted a continuance for a week and a half. When we reconvened, Mr. Smith was still not represented, and Mr. Johnson seemed to have both barrels loaded on behalf of Mrs. Jones.

THE EVIDENCE

"Mr. Johnson," I began, "we continued this hearing from ten days ago..."

"Yes, your honor," Johnson basically interrupted. "I have some photographs to show the court demonstrating that Mrs. Jones has substantially cleaned up the property, and…"

"Well, Mr. Johnson, I'll look at those in a moment, but first I'll hear from the Plaintiff," I said. Johnson sat down.

Plaintiff

Smith was not delighted to be delayed yet another week and a half in getting a messy tenant out of what turned out to have been his recently deceased mother's house. He testified that he showed Jones through the house in August and that Jones immediately liked the place. What prompted him to say, "No pets," he didn't say, but he made a point of telling the Court that he had made that condition clear to Jones when he showed her the property.

Mr. Smith continued, saying that he brought a lease over late in August and met Jones at the house. She and he both signed it. She paid him the security deposit and first month's rent and took possession for a day or so in August with no charge. Since then she had paid her rent faithfully. But late in September, Smith went by the house and saw that Jones had already erected a fence around the back and front yards, had numerous dogs enclosed, had an old car—vintage 1960-something—off to one side that appeared to be undrivable, and that there were boxes, open and unopened, household items and toys, some of which appeared to him to have been discarded, lying around the entire property. Smith said he called Jones later and told her she would have to remedy all these things if she was to stay there. He said she promised she would do so.

However, she didn't, he said, and so he filed for eviction. He showed a copy of the lease to the Court, and it was received without objection. Paragraph 5 addressed the neatness of the property, and paragraph 10 prohibited pets without written permission. Smith also had photos, which he had taken two days ago, showing that even after the continuance, Jones had not cleaned up the property. Smith implied that if he had ever had intentions of letting her cure her breach of lease and his dropping the eviction proceeding, that was off the table, now.

The Court now asked Smith to recall that he had said he told Jones she could not have pets. "Tell me again exactly what you said on that subject," I said. I wanted to see if he had said anything that might have implied to Jones that he meant "inside the house." But Smith said he told Jones simply, "No pets." Since the precise wording of the lease was, "No pets, without written permission," it was clear to me that the lease meant no pets at all, inside or out.

Smith had taken no more than about three minutes to make his case, and the Court asked if Johnson had any questions of him.

"Mr. Smith, you're a good fellow, aren't you?" said Johnson. Smith looked confused. Why was Jones's attorney asking him this? After fumbling for words a bit, however, he said he guessed so.

"You're a community minded citizen, aren't you?" said Johnson. Believing he must be only helping his own cause by agreeing, Smith said he was.

Johnson then showed Smith several photos depicting holes in floors and walls, clearly inside a house, and asked him if he recognized them. Smith said he did not. He did not believe the pictures were of the inside of 100 Country Lane. Johnson did not lay any foundation for the pictures and did not move them into evidence. Johnson asked if Smith had not in fact gotten multiple calls from Jones to fix things about the house, and that he had not responded. Smith looked bewildered, and the Court believed it was not an act. He had no idea what attorney Johnson was talking about. Smith said Jones called about the washing machine and that he had gone right over there and had it fixed. She hadn't made any other calls to him.

As if he had won some victory, Johnson pronounced his cross examination finished and sat down. I made sure Smith had given all the testimony he wanted to, and he had. It was Travis Johnson's show, now.

Defendant

"Mrs. Jones—Lana" Johnson began, "up until a few months ago you lived with your husband in a house the two of you were buying, didn't you?" Jones's face became contorted in a silent expression of anguish that looked something like one of the two theater masks, and she moved her mouth but no sound came out. "I'm sorry, Lana, I know this is difficult. You had a house, didn't you?" Lana Jones finally worked out an inarticulate "yes."

"Your husband is a plumber, isn't he? And he does some electrical work, too, doesn't he?" Nods. "And your husband lost his job, didn't he?" said Johnson, to which Jones managed another agonized "yes" through a contorted face. "And between you, you couldn't keep up the mortgage payments, isn't that right?" Another nod and an unintelligible sound followed. "And then the bank foreclosed, didn't they?" At the reminder of this awful, recent event, Jones almost howled her assent and sobbed loudly.

"I'm sorry, Lana, I know this is hard for you. Take a moment if you need it before we go on."

I looked over at Mr. Smith. The look of bewilderment was back. His wife, who had accompanied him, sat back in the gallery looking disgusted.

Johnson continued, "Mrs. Jones, where did your husband go about that time?"

Jones, not quite composed yet, broke down completely again and blubbered something that sounded like, "eead-da-go-o-o-." Her husband had to go.

"Where did he go?" She couldn't speak. Johnson led his witness and I allowed it. "He went to Afghanistan, didn't he, to pursue work?" Jones nodded and managed a sound that resembled yes.

"And you had to find a place to rent, didn't you." Yes. "And it was not as nice as where you had lived before, was it?" Jones seemed to regain her composure fairly rapidly and said no. Johnson continued, "That's when you found this little house Mr. Smith was renting, wasn't it?"

By this time, Jones was fully recovered, and she said, "Yes. I saw it and I thought it was perfect, and I told him I would take it."

"And how much rent was it?" It was $650 per month. "But it wasn't a perfect house, was it?" There followed a brief recitation of various problems with the house that Jones discovered when she moved in. Johnson prompted her, "And did you tell Mr. Smith about these problems?" Jones said she had told Smith about several things and that he never did anything about them at all. In particular, she said she had a problem with several outlets. She plugged things in and sparks flew. Johnson showed the Court a picture of a burned outlet. There was nothing in the photograph to indicate where it was, and Johnson did not ask Jones to testify as to where the outlet was. In fact, he laid no foundation at all for the photographic evidence, and the Court let the exhibit sit on the bench without entering it at this point.

"And when did you have this problem with the outlet?" Johnson asked. It was obvious to the Court that Johnson was trying to lay the groundwork for a defense that Smith as landlord was in material breach of the lease himself from day one, and therefore the Defendant should prevail. Jones said it was the day she moved in.

Something about the way she answered the question rang wrong in the Court's ears. I wasn't certain that she was lying, but I believed she was, let us say, mis-remembering, just as I believed her opening testimony was, let us say, dramatically enhanced.

Johnson moved on. "Now, Lana, your husband, as you said, is in Afghanistan, isn't he?" And to this and the next few leading questions, Jones said yes. "He's a plumber, but he isn't in the military, right? But he works in support of the military. And he's over there serving his country just as much as if he were in the military, isn't he. And he helps prepare places where our soldiers go and serve, fighting for our country, right? And you're proud of him, aren't you? And he's not at home to be able to help you with all these things that have to be done when you move into a new place, is he?" (This was the tie-in to the case, in Johnson's attempt to make this foray relevant.) "But when he comes home, he's going to be able to do some of these plumbing and electrical things that you can't do, isn't he? And he's going to be able to help you set up things you had to pack up and move, isn't he? But right now, he's serving his country, isn't he." Yes, yes, yes. I half expected him to play the National Anthem for background music.

Johnson milked the Defendant's husband's patriotism for a little bit more effect and then moved on to other matters.

"Now, Mrs. Jones, you worked hard to clean up your yard, didn't you?" Yes. "Are these pictures you took of your yard late yesterday afternoon?" Johnson showed Jones a stack of 8.5 x 11 sheets of paper, printed edge to edge on an inkjet printer, depicting her yard from various perspectives. Jones confirmed they were the pictures she had taken, and Johnson prompted her to testify that the boxes were cleared away and that things were relatively neat, and that she believed the looks of the place should satisfy Mr. Smith. Johnson showed the pictures to Smith, and departed from his direct questioning to chat with Smith about the pictures. I allowed the informal breach of protocol in keeping with the relaxed rules of magistrate court, and Smith said, somewhat reluctantly, that while he had seen the property two days ago and it didn't look that clean, apparently in just one more day, Jones had gotten things cleaned up enough to pass muster. Smith was clearly afraid that this weakened his case.

"Lana, what about the car? Do you have a junk car?"

"No," Lana said, "it's a classic."

"So it's not a junk car? But have you moved it?" Johnson asked.

"Yes," said Jones. "It's gone." Johnson produced a photograph of the place in the yard where the car once sat. He showed it to Smith. Still he didn't ask for any foundation testimony for the photo. In fact, he never did. Eventually, I asked Jones who took the photos, if she used a film or digital camera, if any editing had been done on the images, and if her testimony was that the photos fairly and accurately depicted what they represented—standard foundation. Only then did I admit into evidence these and the other photos Johnson asked to be labeled as exhibits.

"Now, Lana, let's talk about the neighborhood. It's out at [such and such] crossing, isn't it? And perhaps the Judge knows where it is, but is it a nice neighborhood?" Jones demurred. "So, are you saying it isn't exactly safe? What happens there?" To this question Jones described roving groups of hoodlums, frequent calls by neighbors to the police, and break ins. In fact, she said, prompted by Johnson, someone had come right up to one of her windows one night and cut the screen. Johnson produced a picture of a cut window screen. Johnson showed the picture to Smith before asking that it be labeled. Smith said he didn't think the window was on his rental house at all. [While I could have asked him if he objected to the admission of the evidence, I declined. Personally, I didn't need to be picky about this exhibit since I saw it for what it was anyway.]

Johnson didn't miss a beat, but continued with his client. "So your dogs would help protect you in a dangerous neighborhood, isn't that right?" Between the lines, I read that Johnson's argument was that Mr. Smith's rental house was situated in a place of crime where it would be unconscionable to prohibit a tenant's owning outside dogs. Johnson took the testimony no further on this point, however, and in fact, never completed the argument, if he ever intended to. Apparently, he hoped merely planting the idea was enough.

"Lana, you're a dog lover, aren't you." Johnson began another series of leading questions. The Court ruminated on this tactic for a moment and realized that Travis Johnson had known he was not going to be facing an attorney for the other side in this hearing, and he was leading his own witness on direct examination, to which an opposing attorney would have objected immediately and repeatedly if necessary. But knowing there would be no attorney to object, he was taking his chances that the Judge would not enter an objection on behalf of the *pro se* plaintiff. And, in fact, I didn't. I would not have let Johnson lead his witness before a jury, but I didn't bother stopping up my own ears, because from Johnson's first rush of questions, I had figured out his strategy, and I wanted to watch him work it out merely for the interest value. I knew the case was about one thing: whether or not Lana Jones had violated her lease and refused to cure the breach. Unless Johnson succeeded in producing some evidence that the lease was not valid or that it was signed under duress or that Smith had agreed to Jones's having the dogs after the lease was signed—none of which Johnson suggested at all—then this was more distraction.

In fact, although Jones alleged in her Answer that she had a witness to Smith's allowance of her dogs, she didn't produce one. In addition, in her Counterclaim, filed by her attorney at the last moment, she alleged that Smith had rushed her through the signing of the lease so as to keep her from realizing that she was agreeing that the house could be sold out from under her at any time. (This disclosure was in paragraph 7 of the lease.) But Johnson never pursued this counterclaim at all.

Jones said she had owned multiple dogs over the years and that she and her husband raised and sold dogs, that she had several kennels at her previous house. Prompted to tell the Court more, she rattled off cutesy names and dripped with affection about her canine brood.

"But you realized that when you moved, you might have to part with all the dogs, didn't you?" Suddenly near tears again, Jones said yes. "And even now, if the Judge were to order you to get rid of the dogs, you would, wouldn't you?" Jones nodded, and the Judge realized that Johnson was planting the suggestion that the Court could come up with a free wheeling solution that involved injunctive relief and ignored the nature of the case as well as the Plaintiff's rights.

"And have you tried to find a place for the dogs to go?" Jones had put ads on *craigslist.com* since the court last convened. "So if the Court were to give you thirty days or sixty days to get rid of the dogs [hint, hint], you would comply, wouldn't you. You would find good homes for Daisy and Duke and all your other precious dogs, wouldn't you? And you would do what the Judge says, wouldn't you?" Yes, yes, yes.

Johnson looked down at his notes, looked back up at me, paused a second, then announced that the Defendant rested. Johnson was not an inexperienced lawyer, so why he appeared to be wrapping up things before Mr. Smith had been given the opportunity to cross examine, I didn't know, but I asked Smith if he had any questions. No, he said, but he had some statements. I had reserved his right to offer rebuttal testimony, so I invited him to do so.

Smith only wanted to repeat his denial that he had neglected to fix anything he had been asked to attend to at the rental house. I then asked Mr. Smith if Mrs. Jones had made any of her requests in writing. No, she hadn't.

Smith was finished, Johnson had one small question on re-cross, and then testimony was over. I told the parties I would take five minutes or so to deliberate and then return. In fact, I knew what I would say. All I wanted to do was to write out precisely how I was going to say it.

THE JUDGMENT

1. The complaints of the Plaintiff about a junk car and generally messy appearance have been addressed to what would appear to be the satisfaction of the Plaintiff, as the parties stipulated. However, upon the preponderance of the evidence, the Court finds that the Defendant's addition of a fence without permission violates paragraph 5 of the lease, and her possession of dogs, from the very first and to this moment, violates paragraph 10. Despite what may have been discussed prior to the signing of a written lease about the possibility of pets outside, the written lease controls the agreement. It states without making any exception, "No pets without written permission," and there is no other written permission amending the lease to allow dogs.

I looked up as I began zeroing in on the dogs, and noted that Jones's facial expression, which during testimony had gone from wretched to harried to worried to sorrowful, was now cold, hard and full of scorn, and I believed it was for me. I had not bought any of what she and her attorney were selling. I continued:

2. In other words, it all comes down to the dogs. And while the Plaintiff may well have been satisfied if by the time of this hearing the dogs and the fence had been removed, by the Defendant's admission they have not. Therefore, the court

must find that the Defendant is material breach of the lease.

3. It is not within the authority of the Court in an eviction case to grant the tenant extra time: that is in the purview of the Landlord. It is not in the Court's province to extend this matter further by issuing an order for the Defendant to dispose of the dogs by a given date, and to order either explicitly or implicitly that the landlord accept those conditions. The Court is called upon either to approve or disapprove the Application for Ejectment. The basis of that decision is a finding upon the question of whether or not the tenant is in material violation of the lease, and the Court has made a finding in that regard.

The Court therefore renders Judgment for the Plaintiff and approves the Application for Ejectment. A Writ of Ejectment will be issued upon Plaintiff's payment and application for that writ, and will be posted in due course by the Constable of this Court.

When I asked if there were any questions, Travis Johnson rose and added, "Your honor, I would like to state on the record that Mrs. Jones would very much like to stay in the property, and that she is willing to make an arrangement with Mr. Smith right now for a deadline to have the dogs and the fence removed. We believe it can be done within the week. I realize your honor doesn't have to respond to that, and that your honor will not order Mr. Smith to agree to such terms. I just believe that Mr. Smith knows that Mrs. Jones has paid her rent, and I think he would rather have a renter who pays than to be trying to find another one so soon. And it's Christmas, and I know Mr. Smith doesn't want to be putting anybody out at Christmas—"

"As I said," I broke in, "giving more time is up to Mr. Smith. I'll leave that to his good graces."

Smith held up a finger and said to me, "Can I respond?" I asked if he really wanted his response to go on the record. He just wanted to ask a question. "If I talk with them about doing that, does your order still stand?" I saw what his concern was and I explained to him:

"Mr. Smith, you do not have to pay the fee for the Writ of Ejectment today. If you want to work with Mrs. Jones for a week or ten days at most, and things work out, fine: we'll close the case. If you come to an agreement about the dogs but then things don't work out, you can take out the Writ. I will let the case remain open and the order stand for a reasonable but short amount of time." I tapped the gavel and made my way out, while Smith and Johnson began talking about the possibility of setting a time limit of just a few days for the fence and dogs to disappear.

An observer of the trial remarked to me later that Mr. Johnson seemed bizarre and that she wouldn't dare hire him as her lawyer. I answered that Mr. Johnson was retained at the last minute to represent someone who, as he must have known by even a brief look at the facts, didn't have a case at all. He did what any good lawyer would have done: obfuscate. And while he was obfuscating and misdirecting, he threw in creative, alternative resolutions. Finally, he proposed settlement, even after his client lost. In short, he fought for his client tooth and nail.

Unfortunately, it was all for nought. Smith took out the Writ, and a week after the trial, just before the Christmas holidays, the Court's Constable executed a set out of the woman's possessions. She was already packing her things in a U-Haul truck when the Constable arrived, and she refused to let the Plaintiff's crew come in the house, threatening them with various things if they tried. She was loud and belligerent, shouting at Smith and ranting about how she was being evicted only on "a technicality." The Constable called the Judge to update me. I advised him to use his sound discretion in handling the matter. The Constable called in a sheriff's deputy, who helped him calm things down. When Jones finished, she "dug out" of the driveway in the truck and barreled down the street recklessly. The deputy shook his head, got in his cruiser, turned on his blue lights and took off after her.

Merry Christmas.

12

FAMILY PAINTING

Perhaps second only to the common wisdom to never lend money to relatives is the oft repeated rule in business never to hire family. It's a bit tough to follow that rule in a family operated business. But a man or woman in the business of building widgets should run away from the idea of hiring his or her brother or niece or cousin, even as a subcontractor. It's a recipe for trouble.

In the following case, second cousins squabbled about a business arrangement that ended badly. No matter how it had been decided, both parties really lost, because something more precious than money was gone.

THE PLEADINGS

Leon Smith filed a Summons and Complaint with the Court asking for $1,600.00 as fair compensation for painting he performed for Defendant Jones Construction Co., on a contract in which Jones dismissed Smith before the job was finished. Defendant Jones Answered that Smith's suit was frivolous, without saying why. To this general denial Jones added a Counterclaim for $2,400.00 for damages to be described and proven at trial, and saying, "We here at Jones Construction cannot let Smith get away with wasting the Court's time, so we're countersuing."

THE EVIDENCE

Leon Smith sat alone at the Plaintiff's table and Sylvester Jones sat across the aisle with his only witness, Pete Green, his foreman. The tension was palpable between the two sides as the Court began the hearing and swore everybody in at once.

Plaintiff

Smith began by telling a simple story that he and Jones saw each other at a motorcycle shop in Bigville and after a short conversation Jones agreed to hire Smith as a painting subcontractor. Jones's construction business built new houses, and he had a house of some 2,400 square feet at 101 Lovely Lane to be painted pronto. Smith said he and Jones agreed to a price of $3,400.00.

Smith and his small crew of men started work the following day, he said. Without saying anything about the time frame or giving any details about the house or the actual painting done, Smith skipped to the point at which Jones dismissed him from the job. He said, "For some reason or another, Sylvester didn't want me to finish. He had his foreman come out there and say, 'We want you to leave. And don't come back.'" Smith said he was confused and didn't understand why Jones was not going to allow him to finish. "We were, I would say, 95% finished. Well, maybe not 95%, but more like 90% done. We could have finished in a day, I'd say." The Court asked how many hours he estimated he and his men had worked on the house. About eighty, Smith guessed.

I was curious about his expression, "for some reason or another," and I asked him if there were any particular reason given him for his dismissal. Smith shrugged disingenuously and said in a round about way that he didn't know.

The Court asked Smith about his written Complaint, in which he had stated that the contract was for $3,600.00. He confirmed it was. Then he said, no, it was for $3,400.00. He wasn't sure. Finally, he settled on $3,400.00. The Court asked what he had been paid. Jones had paid him $1,200.00 up front. And how much was he asking in damages? He figured that if he were about 90% finished, Jones would have had to spend about $800.00 more to get the painting completed. Subtracting $800.00 from the $2,200.00 he would have been paid if he had been allowed to finish as contracted, he came up with $1,600.00 in damages.

The Court's calculator silently ticked away at the numbers. The $800.00 figure actually represented something just less than 25%

of the total contract amount. Had Smith originally estimated to himself that he had been 75% finished with the painting? Smith continued his testimony:

"I don't understand why Sylvester didn't come out there himself and tell me. He had Pete fire me instead. Sylvester never came out there, and I didn't hear from him about any complaints. I thought things were going all right. I don't understand." Smith sank back in his chair somewhat sullenly, as if convinced already that he was not going to win his case. Was that all of his testimony, I wanted to know? "Yeah, pretty much." I assured Mr. Smith that he would have the right to give reply testimony later if necessary, and then I turned to Mr. Jones for any cross examination. That's when the holes in the story began to be filled in rapidly, and the tale got considerably longer.

Jones began by assailing Smith's lack of recall of the contract amount. How was the agreement reached? Did they shake hands? Did Smith shake Pete's hands or Sylvester's? None of the answers was significant, apparently, but Jones was energetic and adversarial and seemed to be trying to put Smith off balance. He had obviously watched some TV courtroom programs.

"When did you actually begin the job?" Jones wanted to know. Smith finally agreed that it was not the next day as he had said, but three days later that he began. "Did you always follow directions?" Jones asked. Smith said he had. "Always? And remember you swore to tell the truth," countered Jones. Smith repeated that he had followed instructions, but he didn't use Jones's description of 'always.'

Now, Jones got to one of the key problems he had encountered with Smith's crews' performance. "Do you remember that we told you not to use any paintbrush on the trim?" Jones engaged in some circumlocution but finally said yes, that was the direction he was given. "So, we told you to spray the trim, correct?" Yes, that was correct. "And did my foreman find your men painting trim with a brush one day?" Smith launched into a description of what he remembered as the incident he presumed Jones was referring to. Jones interrupted him, as he often did throughout the entire cross examination: "Just yes or no. Did Pete come in one day and see that your guys were using a brush on the trim? Yes or no!" Smith continued his story where he had left off. "Yes, or no," Jones repeated, volume upped a notch or two.

The Court interrupted in a level voice. "Mr. Smith, I understand you want to tell how things happened, but the question seems not to need anything more than a simple answer. If Mr. Jones doesn't ask you such questions as will allow you to tell what you see as the whole truth, you will have the opportunity to give reply testimony later to fill in the details." That seemed to satisfy Smith for the moment, although he continued to resist the idea of saying just yes or no, mostly to avoid giving Jones what he wanted, I believed.

"And what did you do personally, Leon? When you were there?" Jones asked. Smith bristled a bit and protested that he was on the job site most of the time, and that he rolled most of the ceilings and walls. He estimated that he painted for about fifty hours. He had some other jobs going, and he was sometimes away from 101 Lovely Lane. "Your honor, he was almost never there," Jones tried to testify. I instructed Jones to use this time to ask questions only. (During the course of their respective cross examinations, I gave this instruction to both parties probably two dozen times.)

Jones then peppered Smith with questions about whether or not Smith had told foreman Green to tell his crew, not Smith himself, if there were a problem—which would have implied that Smith was not often on the site. Jones asked about Smith's problems with his men, financial difficulties with paying them, and other grievances on the site. I interrupted to ask what relevance such questions had to the specific complaint. Jones promised to show how they related, then didn't, but moved on before it became an issue for the Court.

"Did the contract include materials and labor? Jones asked. Yes, the contract was for both paint and painting. Jones then asked if he himself had ever bought and delivered paint to the job site. Smith remembered that he did. "Do you know how much I spent on that paint?" Smith didn't. "Do you know how much you bought? How much did you spend—do you have the total of the receipts?" Jones continued. Smith tried to explain something about his purchases and Jones interrupted with another demand to "answer yes or no!" This time, it was Jones's turn to be chastened:

"Mr. Jones," I said, "Mr. Smith is the adverse party here, but I have not declared him to be a hostile witness. That means he doesn't have to answer just yes or no to every question. It seems you have phrased your question in a way that backs him into a corner. I will allow him to give a fuller answer." Jones was, as both men were throughout, respectful to me, and dutifully acknowledged Smith's right to continue to answer at length.

Jones then entered some pictures into evidence for Smith to identify. Smith described the first as one of the bedrooms with a wavy line between colors on a wall. The other was of a door with paint peeled off a large area. Jones's terse questions did not give Smith the opportunity to tell the entire story behind each situation, and the Court allowed Jones to move on quickly to other things. Then abruptly, Jones looked at his notes and announced that he was finished with his questions.

Smith wanted to give some additional, direct evidence, and he told how his men had painted the doors as they were all brought into the closed garage for spraying. At some point, he said Foreman Green had knocked them over. He said Green had been told not to raise the garage door, but that he did so from the outside and the garage door had caught on some of the freshly painted room doors and knocked them over. The doors had then stuck together, damaging the paint. So it wasn't his fault.

Jones got to cross examine and asked why Smith had just let the doors sit there? The picture he had taken after ordering Smith off the site illustrated his point, that Smith had not repainted the doors. Smith raised his voice and said that was one of the things he would have fixed, the very day he was relieved of his job, "But you didn't give us a chance. We could have fixed all that stuff probably in a day."

Defendant

With no more questions on cross, it was now Jones's turn to present a defense, and he rose and began a forceful tale of a lesson learned. He and Leon were third cousins, he said. From details that came out later, it appears they were actually first cousins twice removed, but I let it go. Few people understand how the relationships are actually defined. The point is that they were family, and *that*, said Jones, was his mistake—hiring family. He admitted he had heard you should never hire family, but he did it because he had always liked Leon and he knew that Leon had been in the painting business a long time—thirty years, according to Smith himself.

From the first, however, Jones said there were problems. The first, and one of the greatest to Jones, was the fact that Smith's men painted some of the woodwork with brushes. Jones backtracked to describe the reputation he had acquired in his construction business. One of the features of his homes was the "matte" appearance of the trim, the chair rails, door frames, windows and other woodwork, an effect produced by spraying them rather than brushing the paint on. He said he was very explicit in directing Smith not to use any brushes. However, he came to the site one day and discovered that his men had painted numerous portions of chair rails and a few doors with brushes. He described how difficult it was to redo these surfaces and eliminate the brush marks. In the end, it was necessary for the trim to be thoroughly rubbed, which meant to be sanded, in order to remove the brush stroke marks.

Jones went on to describe how he appeared at the site every day and almost never found Smith there. "He didn't supervise his men," Jones said. "That's why they used brushes. He wasn't there." Jones also testified that the special paints he used for deeply colored walls required particular techniques that Smith did not employ. He never described the techniques, and Smith did not contradict the testimony, so the Court was never enlightened on the techniques, but apparently Smith had no defense against this complaint. Jones, and later his witness Green, referred to splotchy walls as evidence that Smith had not done the painting as directed.

Another sticking point was the garage, which Jones said he told Smith at the outset to paint first and to be finished with it, because the owner wanted to move some things into it. Jones said Smith dillydallied about the garage and had to be reminded several times to finish it. That required Smith to finish painting the doors, which were sprayed in the closed garage, and then to apply all coats of paint to the garage itself. The owner made several trips to check on the progress and at one point became very upset with Jones Construction Co. Sylvester Jones was quite concerned about his reputation as a builder, and considered Smith's heel dragging as affecting the kind of recommendations he would get from this owner. When the incident with the doors took place, foreman Green reported it to Jones, and Jones finally decided Smith would have to go.

The Court was also ready to go, as it was five o'clock and the Defendant showed no signs of stopping. I asked how much longer he anticipated his case would take. He believed about fifteen or twenty minutes. Using my reality calculator, I expanded his estimate by a factor of 2.5, and I told the parties we would recess for the day. There being no time left in the week when we could reconvene, I continued the case until next week at the same time.

When we gathered again, oddly enough Sylvester Jones seemed somewhat sedate, as if he had wound himself up the week before and couldn't quite get his steam back now. He knew where he had left off, but didn't have any energy and seemed to lack purpose as he tried to pick back up. Consequently, he was finished in about five minutes.

Conversely and surprisingly, Leon Smith, who had appeared timid and defeated the week before, had built up the steam Jones had expended in tooting his horn. Smith charged into cross examination as if he were a young lawyer. Smith, about sixty years old and having, as I surmised, no more than a high school education, had obviously done his share of court television watching, too. He got up, walked around, asked pointed questions, phrased himself nicely, and went after Jones on numerous little points.

At the heart of Smith's questions was why Jones waited so long to pull him off the job. "If we were doing such a bad job," he said, "why would you wait until we were 90% done to fire me? Why not do it the first week, or before we finished most of the house?"

"Because you were family," Jones said insistently. "I thought you would come through. I really didn't want to take you off, but I finally had to."

None of the rest of what Smith asked really addressed relevant evidentiary matters, but it had the effect of embroiling the two in a back and forth repartee—as had happened frequently throughout the previous three hours of the hearing on its two days. It prompted me to break in.

"Gentlemen, I remind you that the purpose of these questions and answers is to bring out testimony for my benefit, not to settle an argument between the two of you. Do not argue with each other during cross examination. You [Smith] ask questions only, and you [Jones] just answer them. That's all." Both men nodded cooperatively.

Smith was finished soon and Jones called his witness, foreman Pete Green. Green described the incident in the garage, but only far enough for the Court to realize that he had not been there himself, but had learned of it from his assistant, who was there at the site with him that day. Similarly, Smith had not witnessed the doors falling himself, but had learned of it from his men as well. What happened after that was clear, however. Smith's men expected Jones's man to pick up the doors, which he didn't, and neither did Smith's men. In consequence, the doors stuck together and were pulled apart only when they were nearly dry, explaining the large places where paint was peeled off.

Green was the witness who satisfied the Court that the extent and aggregation of problems on the job site warranted Jones's cancelling the contract with Smith. Unfortunately, Green also undermined his boss's case, though I was certain he did not know it at the time. Jones violated the cardinal rule of cross: don't ask a question to which you don't already know the answer. Trying to answer Smith's earlier question about why Jones had waited so late to dismiss him, Jones asked Green why a contractor would be reluctant to replace a "sub."

"Because," said Green, it's more trouble. And you lose time. And—" and he continued with a detailed explanation and launched into an illustration. The Court interrupted and said that the testimony appeared to have wandered into irrelevant and time consuming detail that I didn't really need to hear. But just as I interjected my remark, Mr. Green was saying, "And besides, often a new subcontractor will charge even *more.*" That was his most telling piece of evidence, as I made clear in my Judgment later.

Smith adopted the same, aggressive techniques in cross examining Green, clearly impressed with himself. While it was interesting to watch him, time was wasting. But shortly, he made an end of it and sat down.

With some trepidation, I asked if either man wanted to sum up his case, and both surprisingly took only about thirty seconds to do so, and we were done.

Having another matter in the court after theirs, I thanked the parties for their presentations and their respect of the Court, and announced that I would render Judgment within forty-eight hours by mail. I prefer not to delay Judgments, but will when time constraints force me to.

JUDGMENT

From the greater weight of the testimony, the Court finds as follows:

1. The Plaintiff and Defendant did have an oral contract under which the Plaintiff would paint Defendant's new home construction at 101 Lovely Lane for $3,400.00. At the time the Defendant cancelled the contract between the two, the Defendant had paid Plaintiff $1,200.00 towards the total.
2. Jones made his performance standards clear to Smith. Those

standards included: instructions not to use brushes; spray techniques with special paints; and rubbing all surfaces after coats. Plaintiff substantially breached the contract: by failing to abide by each of these standards in several instances; by failing to supervise persons performing the painting work such that they in turn failed to abide by these standards; and by failing to meet deadlines made explicit from the outset of the job.

3. The amount of the contract Plaintiff completed was not 90% or more as Plaintiff claimed, as shown by the amount of work that was required to correct defects and complete the job as originally contracted. The evidence suggests that from a time perspective, at least as much work as had already been performed was left to be performed, in order to correct and complete.

4. The Defendant's cancelling the contract with Mr. Smith was in itself evidence of the extent of problems with the job. The Court has every reason to conclude that Mr. Jones's business has not prospered and grown by capricious firing of subcontractors for little or no cause.

5. Defendant was damaged perhaps as much by the delay and negative report of this incident as by any moneys he subsequently spent on the painting itself. Considering this damage to reputation and delay in scheduling, the Plaintiff's breach was material.

6. Therefore, Defendant was justified in cancelling the contract and refusing to pay Plaintiff the remainder of the contract amount.

7. There is insufficient evidence, however, to support the Defendant's claim of $2,690.89 in damages. When a contract is cancelled with one party and that party is not allowed to cure a breach, damages to a contractor may not be a simple matter of adding up what he then pays a third party to complete the work.

8. Although half or more of the originally contracted job had to be performed, no evidence was presented that figured in the

contribution to the next subcontractor of materials already purchased, or that evaluated the scope of the work performed by the next subcontractor as against that performed by Smith. Defendant alleged that the job required almost total redoing by the final subcontractor secured to do the work. However, Defendant's witness's testimony conflicted with itself on this point. In fact, the witness specifically said that one reason a contractor is reluctant to replace an original subcontractor is that a subsequent subcontractor may actually charge more. That possibility in itself may have accounted for a substantial amount of Defendant's expenses after he released Smith. Lacking key evidence to show that comparing the final subcontractor's work and charges to Mr. Smith's work and charges was not comparing apples to oranges, the Court finds the Defendant's evidence of Jones's damages not to be compelling.

9. The Defendant's Counterclaim relies on this insufficient evidence and therefore cannot stand.

In the matter of the Plaintiff's Complaint, therefore, on the basis of the foregoing facts as articulated in items 1-6, the Court finds for the Defendant and wholly dismisses the Complaint.

In the matter of the Defendant's Counterclaim, on the basis of the facts articulated in items 7-9, the Court dismisses the Counterclaim in its entirety.

Nobody won. Even if one had, both would still have lost. It's family.

13

HOME DEFENSE

Few things cause the average person to feel anxious and afraid like the prospect of losing his home. The condition of homelessness in America has come into focus in recent years because of the increased numbers of people who for one reason or another have lost or just left their places to live. It's a strange fact that some few people actually choose to live on the streets. The greater number of homeless didn't set out to be homeless but they chose paths of little education, lots of drinking, drug use or crime, that led to joblessness or squandered resources, and they lost their homes through eviction, foreclosure, imprisonment, or just losing their breadwinner. A few people have no homes for no real fault of their own at all.

In my experience, I see people who are satisfied with the barest shelter and make a habit of moving from place to place frequently with little more than a bag and a box. Most people, however, have considerably more possessions and were raised in a secure environment where home was a thing of relative permanence. Facing the sudden and imminent possibility of losing their very place to eat and sleep will bring out the basic instinct of human beings to defend themselves against whoever is threatening them.

In the following case, tensions rose on both sides of a landlord-tenant relationship. By the time it came to court, not only the parties but the judge as well was concerned about self defense.

THE PLEADINGS

Max Smith did business with the court now and then for years. He was known by court personnel as one of the odder persons in the community. One would never have guessed that this short, round, gruff, burr-headed, red faced, wild eyed man who barely ever spoke in complete sentences and gave the impression of having either no education or being only half in his right mind was in fact one of the richer persons in town. He was known to flash a four inch roll of hundred dollar bills on occasion. He owned small rental properties throughout the community, mostly with small houses on them, and he drove a battered old pickup truck around at the first of the month and collected rents.

Mr. Smith's daughter Lynn had helped him for a number of years since she had become an adult. In fact, she lived at home well into her thirties and managed a good part of his business for fifteen years. Often when Max needed to file an eviction, it was Lynn who did the filing. She had no trouble having a cogent conversation, while Max was increasingly deaf and anti-social as well.

Lynn Smith came to the court on December 29 to file an eviction against David Jones and his wife Dana, who lived in one of the Smith's rental properties on Pleasant Road. She appeared unusually flustered. It seems that one of their tenants had threatened to shoot her father between the eyes.

The usual question about whether or not the tenant had paid rent yielded the answer that he had, but that he had two dogs that Max didn't allow, and that they, Lynn and Max, had decided they didn't want to rent to him. Lynn said that when Max had gone by the house, Jones had come out of the house, informed Smith that he had a concealed weapons permit, and had threatened to shoot Max if he didn't get off the property. The predictable argument had ensued and Max had left. Lynn Smith said that on a subsequent occasion Jones had come out of the house and threatened both her father and her sister, who also worked in the family business. The court took the filing and advised the Constable of the possibility that serving the Rule to Show Cause might be dangerous.

In a few days, the Constable returned to the Court's chambers and reported to me that he had served the paper to David Jones. The Constable had a quizzical and somewhat amused look on his face and told me that Mr. Jones was just as nice as he could be. He was a man of about thirty with a young wife and a little baby, and the Constable said he was courteous and made pleasant conversation. He wondered if he had gone to the right house.

In another few days, the tenant, now Defendant Jones, submitted an answer to the suit for possession. Jones told another story, about the dogs, about Smith's actions, and about the nature of the lease. He also complained about landlord Smith's refusing to have the heat fixed. Interestingly, Jones said it was Smith who had threatened to shoot him. Jones asked for a hearing. Since he was not in default in rent, he was entitled to a hearing, and a date was set for late in January, the next available day for trial.

When Max Smith got word of the answer, he came back to the court, this time in person, to request subpoenas for two police officers who had come in response to his or his daughter's calls on two occasions. The court prepared the subpoenas and served them upon the two municipal officers who had responded to the calls.

THE EVIDENCE

As the day of the hearing approached, I directed the court clerk to have an officer operate the security screening booth and to require all persons entering the courtroom that day, except for the two policemen, to pass through. While we do not normally require screening for civil court proceedings, I wasn't going to take any chances that one of two people alleged to have threatened to shoot the other might bring a pistol and make good on the threat, or even take their anger out on the Judge when I ruled in the case. Although I carry my own courtroom security under my robe, I would opt not to need it, if possible.

Fortunately, on the day of trial all parties arrived, passed screening and assembled in the courtroom with no disturbance.

Plaintiff

David and Dana Jones sat at the defendant's table with their baby in a rocking carrier on the floor. I swore in all witnesses at one time and then turned to the Plaintiff for his testimony. Max blurted out something mostly unintelligible except for the words, "Let's just get him out." His daughter Lynn gave me a plaintive look and said she would like to speak for him. I told her I would certainly let her testify as to what she knew personally, but that she couldn't act as his lawyer. Max did not have an incorporated business. If he had, Lynn could have functioned as a non-lawyer representative with the proper authorization. But filing as an individual, Max had to conduct his own case unless he brought a licensed attorney. I would need Max to testify. She understood, but she did have some testimony to present herself, and I began with her.

Lynn said her father had rented to David Jones on December 1, just about two weeks before he then turned around and filed to evict him. Max had met with Jones at the rental house as he was moving in and had collected the first month's rent on that day. She said the terms were $600.00 per month. She then said that she herself came to the house a few days later with a copy of the lease and went over it with Mr. Jones. She saw the dogs and apparently was concerned that they were larger than her father would want in the house. At her mention of dogs during her testimony, apparently the only word that Max had understood, he said, "Dogs! Big dogs. Little dogs, but no big dogs!" and he held up his hands about six to eight inches apart and then about two feet apart in illustration. I asked him to hold his comments until I was ready to hear from him.

Lynn said she took the printed lease back home to make a copy of it for Jones, but that after returning home, "we (she and her father) decided we didn't want to rent to him." So she didn't provide Jones with a copy of the lease.

Did Jones sign it, I wanted to know? Lynn Smith said he did. In fact, I had one page of the signed lease in the pleadings, showing both Max Smith's and David Jones's initials. Max and Lynn Smith had submitted it themselves. It was the page that prohibited dogs without written permission. Knowing that Mr. Jones had contested the validity of this written lease, signed after he had already moved in, I then asked Ms. Smith if at the time Jones signed it she regarded it as valid, since Jones had already taken possession under other terms. What other terms, she asked? I explained that from what she had told me, little more had been agreed about the rental at the time that Jones moved in than that Jones would pay $600.00 per month.

Smith had no answer to the question and seemed confused as to why I had asked it. It was clear that she didn't know exactly what agreement her father had reached with Jones. She went on testifying about several things that then happened in December, including a complaint about the heat and the visit of a repairman and what he said about the heat pump. I sensed this was not information that Lynn Smith had firsthand knowledge of, and I interrupted her.

"Were you there when the repairman came?" She wasn't, but he reported his findings to her. "Is he here in the courtroom today?" I asked. He wasn't. I told Smith she would not be able to report his words if they were meant to prove any fact that had bearing on the case. She seemed flustered, and went on to say that because there was nothing wrong with the heating system—and again I interrupted: "You believe that because the repairman told you so?" She said yes. I disallowed the testimony and told her that if the matter of the heat was important testimony, the repairman would have to be here. She said she had thought he was coming.

Ms. Smith looked at notes and continued, but interrupted herself a couple of times, having realized the rest of what she had to say was inadmissible hearsay. In fact, she had not been with her father when he first met with the Joneses and agreed to let them rent. I had to hear from Max himself about what the oral agreement was, and I told her so. At this point, Max blurted out, "No lease. Just $600.00 a month. Don't want no lease." I assured Mr. Smith that he would get to testify in a few minutes. He grinned semi-toothlessly and sat back.

Whether under an oral lease or legitimately under a written one, the tenant was still covered by the protections of the Landlord-Tenant Act, and so I asked Ms. Smith if she had given written notice to Mr. Jones about the dogs, with a right to cure. She searched and came up with two papers that the clerk showed across the aisle, marked as exhibits, and set on the bench. I inspected them and found them to be two copies of the same paper, namely the court's own Rule to Vacate or Show Cause. I explained that this was not a fourteen day notice about the dogs. Did she know what a fourteen day notice was? She hesitated and then said no.

I reviewed with her the provision in the law that a landlord must give written notice of breach of lease and fourteen days to correct the situation. Then I asked if she knew of the provision in her own lease that required that notice. In fact, the page of the lease she gave the court when she filed for eviction contained not only the paragraph disallowing dogs but also the one requiring a fourteen day notice, and it was lifted directly out of the state statute. She looked blank and said she didn't know about that provision, either, and I believed her. I believed the lease had been copied blindly from some boilerplate she acquired haphazardly. I also wondered how she had managed her father's business for years without knowing about these basic laws. What was curious was that she wanted the Court to take note of the tenant's violating the no-dogs provision but she didn't want to enter the lease as evidence. The conflict was glaring.

Smith added, almost as an afterthought, that Jones had not paid his rent for January. It was now January 30.

I took a question in cross examination from Jones. Jones asked why Smith never gave him back a copy of the written lease. Lynn Smith explained it was because, as she had said, they changed their minds and didn't want to rent to him. Jones asked why and Smith said it was because they had dogs without permission. Jones asked why she didn't say anything about that when she was there and saw the dogs, or why Max himself didn't say he wouldn't allow the dogs when he was there on December 1 and saw them in the house. Smith fumbled a bit and couldn't piece together an exact answer, but Max again interrupted gruffly about big dogs and little ones and held up his hands as before, folding his arms across his belly when he finished, and peering at the Judge as if this whole proceeding was both irritating and unnecessary.

Jones had no more questions and I turned to Selena Smith, the other daughter, who had clearly been itching to talk, though it was difficult to understand her when she finally did, because at barely thirty years old she had no teeth and also talked rapidly and excitedly.

She spun a story about going over to the rental house to work on the gutters, and how Jones came out of the house and told her he hoped she would fall off the ladder. She gave no details of why he would say such a thing, or why Jones would call her "a b__" or a "whore," which she also said he did.

—Before abbreviating the "B" word, Selena feigned (as I believed) reluctance to say it aloud in court. However, from her presentation so far, I detected a crude, rough woman behind a thin facade of someone more gentle. I believed that Selena had provoked David Jones. Otherwise, his outburst at her was inexplicable.

Then Selena said that a few days later she and her father were down the street about three houses away at another rental property, and that Jones had come outside and shouted out threats from his yard. She said she heard him say, "I have a concealed weapon and I will shoot you between the eyes!" That's when she called the police.

Smith didn't have any questions of Selena. I believed his silence probably indicated that he had indeed lost his temper with this woman. Selena turned around to some movement in the courtroom and then informed me that the repairman had arrived and that they would like him to testify.

Repairman Green had come out at the request of Max Smith and had inspected the heat pump at the rental property on Pleasant Road. There was nothing wrong with it. The refrigerant, blower unit, and thermostat all checked okay. He said that Mr. Jones told him it got a couple of degrees cooler at night, however, and they didn't want their baby, in particular, to be cold. Green said the house was about 71 degrees the day he went there. The Court was thinking that would make the house 69 or 68 degrees at night—hardly cold. The Judge's own house was kept at 66 most of the time in the winter.

The testimony of Green seemed unrelated to the Plaintiff's case, but it was clear that Smith wanted Green to be a witness because Jones in his Answer had complained that the landlord had been negligent in addressing heating issues. Smith was taking preemptive steps to defeat Joneses defense.

Hearing about daytime/nighttime differences in temperature, I asked repairman Green if the thermostat was programmable, thinking that the Joneses may have taken possession of a house where the previous occupants had set the nighttime temperature very, very low. But no, the thermostat was digital but had only one range, and it was set on 71. Green said he told Jones the unit may have been going into defrost mode in the dead of the night—the Court was thinking of how bitterly cold it had been for a number of days in that December and that heat pumps unfortunately get frozen over and have to defrost. Green said that while the unit was in defrost mode, the temperature might drop a couple of degrees.

He further said that he made another trip to the residence, again at Max Smith's (daughter's) request, and still found nothing wrong. He told Jones that he might have to catch the unit acting up to analyze a problem, and Jones told him, "Come back at two in the morning and you'll see." Green said he wasn't going to come back at two in the morning just to see if anything might happen.

David Jones cross examined Green, asking him if it was true that he said the house got a lot colder at night. Green insisted that Jones had said "a couple of degrees."

Green was dismissed and the Court asked Ms. Smith if she was ready for the officers to testify. Officer Brown testified that he had responded to a disturbance call with his partner one afternoon in the middle of December. Having been told that Jones was talking about having a gun, Brown went to interview him. There on the rental property, Jones confirmed that he had a pistol, allowed Brown to secure it while they talked, and that Brown ran the serial number as a standard procedure. There was no problem with the weapon. Brown assured Jones that he had a legal right to possess the gun on his property, including property he rented. Officer Brown was apparently satisfied that Jones had not crossed the line with respect to the gun. Evidently he had not pointed or presented it, only warned Max Smith that he was not hesitant to use it to protect his property.

Brown did go over the legally allowable uses of the weapon, however, before returning the gun to Jones and ending the call. The Court asked Brown if he ever determined that Jones had a concealed weapons permit. Brown did not believe so, but he could not recall. Did he write up a report on the call? No.

Jones had no questions for Officer Brown, and Officer Black was called to the stand. Black said he came in response to Selena Smith's call on another occasion, that he talked to Max Smith down the street, and that he also spoke to Jones. He said that he advised both Smith and Jones to stay away from each other and let things cool down. With little more to do on the call, he left. Jones had no questions for Black, either. David Jones was just calmly waiting his turn.

The Court asked Max Smith for his testimony. Cupping his hand to his ear, Max said, "What?" I repeated my request to Lynn Smith, who helped communicate with her father. He then said simply, "Let's just get them out, that's all." I asked what agreement he reached with David Jones when he rented to David and his wife on December 1. Max said only that it was "$600.00 a month and no dogs. Little dogs okay. But they got big dogs." He seemed unable to come up with anything more in the way of testimony.

Again, Jones had no questions. And it was finally his turn to present a defense.

Defendant

David Jones described briefly having met with Max Smith at the rental property the day he moved in. He had given Smith a deposit on November 21. Smith came in the house that December day and collected the rent. Jones said the dogs were there in the room where Smith was, and that Smith told him the little dogs were "okay."

I asked Jones if he and landlord Smith ever discussed a lease, a term of occupancy or anything like that. No, he said. I found it curious that Jones would not have wanted to know how long he could live there, but it was clear from what all parties had said that the oral agreement between the two was for a month to month tenancy. I knew that Smith typically did business this way with his renters, establishing month to month tenancies and being very careful about timely payment of rent.

Jones continued that Lynn Smith came over on December 8 and brought a written lease. He said she told him he couldn't stay in the house unless he signed the lease. Jones told her that her father had said there was no lease to sign. Lynn Smith prevailed upon him, however, and he reluctantly signed the papers. However, he said that Max Smith had told him that the dogs were okay, as long as they weren't big.

At this point, Mr. Jones told the Court he had some pictures of the dogs on his phone that he believed he could find if I wanted to see them. I told him to have his wife look for them while he continued. Jones said that Lynn Smith, whether wholeheartedly or not, told him the little dogs were okay, and that she left promising to bring or send him a copy of the lease he had just signed.

Mrs. Jones now had the photos, and after showing them across the aisle, she showed them to me. There were three pictures of one or both of the dogs, full grown boston terriers, neither of which was over fourteen to sixteen inches in height to the top of their ears.

Jones testified that on the day Selena Smith had described, when she and Max were down the street, he had stood in his yard while Max Smith walked down to the house and appeared aggressive. He said Max was fumbling in his pocket dramatically as if there were something in there he was going to draw out, and that as he came close, he said to David, "I have a gun, and I'm going to shoot you." Smith went inside and didn't engage in any argument. He never saw a gun.

Both men had now alleged threats against their persons with guns. The Court had questions about the timing—it seemed to me, for instance, that Max Smith's threat came after David Jones's threat and mostly as bluster to keep things even. I personally did not believe, however, that Max Smith owned a gun and certainly did not believe that he had a permit to carry one concealed. I had serious doubts that he could have passed the CWP course. However, I didn't need to ask any questions to clear up the matter, because as I saw the case so far, interestingly enough, this bravado on display between the two didn't affect the matter of the eviction action.

Jones then addressed the matter of rent payment. He admitted he hadn't paid rent for January, but said that it was only because when he tried to pay Max Smith personally, Smith wouldn't accept it. This was after Smith had filed for ejectment. Jones said he had the rent on him at that moment in court, and would have mailed it, but that Smith refused to give him an address where he could send it. It wasn't until he was served with the eviction notice that he got an address for Max Smith. (To inform myself of when Jones had notice of Smith's address, I glanced down at the case file and saw that my constable had served Jones on January 7.) Jones had done his homework and referred to state law requiring the landlord to give an address where payments and papers could be served. He also mentioned his knowledge of the law requiring fourteen day notices.

Jones entered a little testimony about his wife and his baby, who had made no sound at all during the hearing, to my great appreciation. Jones didn't overly play on the Court's sympathies, but it was clear that he was there to defend his family's right to stay in a place they rented legitimately, where they deported themselves as good tenants, and for which they had done their best in good faith to pay rent.

Jones had wound up just about all he had to say. I asked if the Smiths had any questions. Interestingly enough, they did not. Lynn Smith looked a bit embarrassed. Selena looked defiant as she had throughout. Max sat with his arms crossed over his belly and just looked put out. The absence of questions suggesting any contradiction or contest to Jones's testimony was telling in this particular case, I thought.

I made sure everyone was finished testifying and took a brief recess and then returned with my decision.

THE JUDGMENT

Mr. Smith's filing asks the Court to evict David and Dana Jones over two issues constituting an alleged violation of the terms of the rental agreement: one was "Animal in the house; no large dogs in the house," and the other was, "Tenant has threatened landlord to shoot him between the eyes." There was no complaint about default in rent, though that became part of Plaintiff's testimony.

The court restricts itself to the consideration of the two complaints pled and makes its decision based on these two complaints only.

1. First, the Court finds that there was no written lease prior to the Joneses' taking possession of the rental property. The agreement was oral, it was for month-to-month tenancy, and it was for rent of $600.00 per month. As part of the agreement, the Joneses were allowed to have their two dogs, which both Max and Lynn Smith initially assessed as sufficiently small.

2. The Court finds that the dogs are in fact not large, relative to all dogs or even relative to the average size dogs commonly possessed by pet owners. The photographic evidence shows dogs whose heads do not even come up to the seat level of the Joneses' sofa. Even going by the oral agreement concerning the dogs, they do not violate the understanding Smith and Jones initially had.

3. The Plaintiff showed the Court a page of a written lease in pleadings. Lynn Smith testified that she took that lease to David Jones and that he signed it. Even though the lease itself is not in evidence, the Plaintiff testified to its existence, although he disavows its controlling authority and clearly wishes to void or ignore it. Plaintiff's witness stated under oath

that the written lease bears the signatures of both the landlord and the tenant. However, it was signed under circumstances that put the landlord in a position of superiority resulting in coercion. It was presented for signature after Jones took possession of the property, and it stated conditions that both added to and differed from the conditions understood by the tenant in the oral agreement.

4. All this being found as fact, the Court will not enforce the written lease. Therefore, the term of one year in the lease is not enforced against landlord Smith, nor is a year guaranteed to tenant Jones. The oral agreement for month to month tenancy is all that exists. No other provision of the written lease, including any restriction on dogs, exists to be enforced.

5. In regard to the landlord's threats to shoot the tenant and the tenant's threats to shoot the landlord, both of which were alleged, the Court finds that neither is specifically a violation of the oral agreement or lease between the two. For that matter, neither threat under these particular circumstances is a violation of the Landlord Tenant Act. The law bars a tenant's disruption of the security or peace of other tenants, but it doesn't address the matter of landlord and tenant themselves having a dispute, even if that dispute involves threats. It is clear to me that Mr. Smith and Mr. Jones have argued, but even vehement arguments are not by themselves cause to evict.

6. Even if Mr. Smith decided to end the tenancy of the Joneses over dogs that were unacceptably large, he would have to comply with the Landlord-Tenant Act in supplying the Joneses with a fourteen day notice to cure, which he did not. And in bringing suit in part over the size of the dogs, he has not shown the court either that the original oral agreement banned dogs the size of the two the Joneses possess, or that the dogs are large, whatever that may mean in context.

The issue of default in rent for January was not pled, and I will not use it to decide this case. As it stands, however, the Court will state the following facts as I find them, in order to give notice to both parties of where the tenancy stands at this moment.

7. By not providing an address to which to send rent, Mr. Smith has frustrated Mr. Jones's attempt to pay it. The Court will not hold Mr. Jones in default for January, since the Smiths' notice of an actual address to which to mail their rent payments was not acquired until January 7, two days after the default date for this month.

8. However, the Joneses now have an address for Max Smith. Their tenancy being month to month, they are required to pay rent for January and for February before February 5 in order not to be in default for February.

9. In a month to month tenancy, the landlord may end tenancy for any reason by giving a thirty day written notice of the end of the rental agreement. The earliest Mr. Smith may do so is this upcoming February 1.

Since no matter of fact relating to the issues pled can be found in Mr. Smith's favor, this particular Application for Ejectment is denied.

Immediately after the hearing, Lynn Smith asked what a thirty day notice should contain. The court clerk simply referred Smith to the statute, and indicated that if she were to give Jones a thirty day notice on February 1, end of tenancy would not be until March 2.

The Smith family marched off to put it in writing. The Joneses had defended their home for another thirty one days at least. After that, they were almost certain to have another address.

If there had been any chance that Smith would not terminate Jones's tenancy at February's end, Jones wiped out that chance with a display of his temper. Though he had indicated in court in January that he had the month's rent in his pocket ready to pay it, he did not, in fact, pay for January. When February 5 came and went, he had not paid for February either. Smith gave him notice on February 1 of the end of tenancy, which would have given Jones until March 2 to exit on his own. But when he defaulted February 5, Smith took out another set of 10-day notice eviction papers, which were served February 14.

Jones did not respond or pay by February 24. Smith delayed in getting a Writ until March 7. The Court's Constable served the writ at 3:10 p.m. that day. He returned the following day a little early to execute the writ if Jones had not vacated on his own.

Jones met the Constable in his front yard and Jones may have been carrying his pistol concealed at the time. He announced with bravado that he had until 3:00 o'clock and that until that time, both the Constable and Mr. Smith, who was with him, would have to get off "his" property.

Jones said, "I believe I might just call the police."

Smith, standing beside and just behind the Constable, said, "Well, he's got a badge."

Jones said dismissively, "Aw, he's nobody."

The Constable replied in a low, even tone, "Careful what you say."

At that, Jones clammed up, and shortly he went to the porch and called the city police on his cell phone.

The Constable verified with me that the hour appointed was 3:10, and he simply waited. Shortly, three officers in two cars arrived, half expecting a pistol duel since they had been to the property many times in the past few months and knew that both Smith and Jones were armed. They soon determined that matters were not so dangerous, and after ascertaining that the Constable had the situation well in hand, they left.

Jones made one more trip away from the house to carry away his last load of small boxes, and then he and his wife left for good. Smith and the Constable went into the house. Rabbit droppings littered the interior, which reeked of pet urine. Jones had also possessed both the two known dogs and a cat as it turned out. Several room doors had been removed from their jambs and were lying here and there, some in the back yard. And Smith cursed from the kitchen, "They done stole my refrigerator." And they had.

If it had not been for the refrigerator, Smith might have let the matter drop, but the theft set him seething again. Jones had not paid his rent for either January or February. Smith filed suit to recover $1,200.00 in rent. He kept the security deposit to pay for damages. And he reported the theft to the police, who referred him to me. I granted the warrant for larceny and Jones was soon picked up.

At his hearing, he pled guilty and I found him so. In passing sentence I told him that since he had refused to pay his rent, I wasn't going to bother ordering him to pay a fine. I wanted him to sit in the County jail for thirty days and cool off. The only alternative, if he should want to choose it, was to enroll in an anger management course with the local court services organization. He sniffed at the idea.

He spent the next month in jail. And since he didn't answer the suit for the $1,200.00, the Court granted Smith a Default Judgment.

14

A Case of the Bottom Line

Occasionally the apparent issues of a Complaint and Answer, while legitimate matters worthy of weighing, in and of themselves, become secondary to some other issue that makes the rest relatively irrelevant.

In the following Summons and Complaint, the detailed issues raised by both Plaintiff and Defendant involving plumbing renovation were eclipsed by a question raised by Defendant almost as an afterthought.

THE PLEADINGS

Smith's Plumbing filed a Summons and Complaint against Darlene Jones for not paying two final invoices representing work Smith performed for Jones at her apartment. Jones had bought a downtown building for her business. The building included an apartment where the owner could live, and she was having several areas renovated including a large walk-in shower and bathroom, and the kitchen area. Smith brought in several persons to perform work beginning in early December. For each particular area of work, he created a separate work order and invoice. His Complaint involved just the last two invoices, both for work in the shower. He claimed Darlene Jones stopped the work and had not then paid him. Total damages: $1,680.00.

Ms. Jones in her Answer said first that she was a legal resident of another state more than three hundred miles away and that she therefore contested the court's jurisdiction. She then listed numerous complaints about Smith's Plumbing including unworkmanlike performance, their having to do and redo certain areas, and an accusation that agents for Smith had stolen tools. She also intimated that the signatures on the two work orders weren't her handwriting.

Jones also filed a Counterclaim alleging that after Smith's

Plumbing failed to complete the job, she had to hire another company to come finish it, at a cost of $350.00.

THE EVIDENCE

At trial, the Court first asked Ms. Jones where she lived at present. She said she lived in the apartment in town during the week but that every other week or so she returned to her home state. The Court was satisfied that she was a resident of this state for purposes of the suit, and the objection to jurisdiction was dispensed with.

Plaintiff

Plaintiff's case consisted almost entirely of testimony from Sam Smith, the sole proprietor of Smith's Plumbing. He said he had discussed Ms. Jones's project with her the first few days in December and gotten right to work. The work involved more than plumbing. Since he had also represented himself to Jones as a licensed contractor, she asked him to replace some door trim with pieces she had bought at a surplus yard and to trim out a microwave enclosure in the kitchen. In the bathroom, the shower tile was to be entirely torn out and redone with new fixtures. Even the backer board behind the tile was to be replaced.

Smith said Jones was hard to work with because she was never satisfied with anything. He claimed all the doing and redoing was the result of her being excessively demanding. After laboring through December, Smith said that around the end of the first week in January several heavy snows halted work by keeping him and his crews from being able to go anywhere. Smith was bonded and had a key to enter the apartment when Jones was out of town, but when they attempted to come back to finish the work after the snow closure, Ms. Jones had changed the locks and told them on the phone that she was pulling them off the job. Smith then billed her for the work with invoices 1234 and 1235 totaling $1,680.00. Jones never paid.

In cross examining Smith, Jones asked him if he had used

backer board behind the shower, as the work order said he would. He said he had. Jones later testified that he had not, but had used common wall board—"sheetrock"—instead.

Jones then asked Smith if he had not offered to do the shower job for a flat $1,000.00, not the $1,400.00 shown in one of the two invoices. He agreed that he had, but that the lower offer was made before another change she ordered and that he had to reconfigure the order and increase the cost.

Smith had little more testimony. He called his one witness, whom he had brought simply to testify about working in the shower. He said the cost was increased by having to reconstruct the framing behind the tile for the soap dish, because the previous framing was out of level by an inch over a one foot span.

Jones had no more questions, and Smith rested.

Defendant

Darlene Jones had been eager for her time to talk. Under oath, she began to tell how Smith had dragged his heels, failing to finish one job before starting another, and how much work was simply not of acceptable quality. She produced photographs of several items including a door frame where the trim was pieced instead of continuous. Another picture showed the microwave insert area, lacking trim, which was the condition she said Smith's men left it in when they turned to other projects. She said she had set a deadline of January 3 for the entire renovation and Smith was significantly behind on that date, which was before the snowstorm Smith said had delayed them.

Jones had the most to say about the backer board in the shower. Apparently from her own internet research as well as conversations with another contractor, she learned that Smith had installed common wall board rather than backer board and that "one never, ever uses sheet rock behind shower tile." (Smith begged to differ when he cross examined.)

Jones showed pictures of the shower illustrating from the color of the board cover that it was sheet rock and not tile backer board. Other pictures showed things she was dissatisfied with.

Finally, Darlene Jones presented her two originals of earlier Smith's Plumbing invoices from December, on which appeared her genuine signatures at the bottom, and suggested that the Court look at the signatures on the two invoices 1234 and 1235 presented by Smith. Jones said she didn't remember signing them, and that they didn't look like her signature, anyway. Quite frequently I hear parties claim they didn't sign the contracts that are at issue in court, and seldom do these claims hold up. Ms. Jones offered as proof of her claim the fact that she managed to sell her house in December and went to her home state on January 3 for the closing and didn't return for a week. She couldn't have signed the invoices, she said, which were dated January 3 and 6. I realized, of course, that the dates on which Smith created the work orders certainly could have been earlier than the dates Jones signed them.

Smith had a few questions in cross, only about the sheet rock/backer board issue and the door trim. Smith insisted that sheet rock is often used behind tile and also said that the trim boards Jones bought and wanted him to use on the door had damaged ends that needed to be cut off and pieced. He said that whoever prepped and painted the trim would be able to cover the spliced area and it would not show.

Counterclaim

Since Darlene Jones had submitted a Counterclaim, the Court now permitted her to proceed with it. Alluding to her need to have the work finished, Jones produced a document, which was shown across the aisle and put on the bench. She said it was an estimate from Acme Construction... and at the word "estimate," I stopped her. There was but one other person in the courtroom, a girl of about twenty whom I believed was observing court as part of course requirements in a college nearby. I asked Jones if Acme was present in the courtroom. No. Had she actually had this work done and paid this bill? No, but this was what it was going to cost.

"I am going to disregard what you have just shown me, because it is inadmissible without a witness here to authenticate it," I said. She didn't understand what constituted inadmissible hearsay, and

I briefly explained. She was disappointed, but did not argue. Was there anything else, I asked, and she shrugged and realized there was nothing else she could say about the Counterclaim.

I asked Smith if he had any response, considering that I had just disallowed the estimate. He realized what my refusal to accept the evidence meant, and he said No.

Smith was done. Jones rested. It was time for summations if they wanted to give them. Many magistrates do not offer parties in civil cases a chance to give summations unless they have attorneys. I always do in Summons and Complaints, even if I have to gently coach a party through and keep him or her focused on argument instead of giving new evidence. I want everyone to feel he has had the opportunity to have his say. I don't want someone to think I muzzled her before she said what she thought made her case.

Smith briefly summed up the same argument he had made, the simple case for being paid for work he did and to which Jones had agreed on the invoices he had submitted to the Court.

Jones was brief as well, asking the Court to consider the photographs, all the areas of poor workmanship, the missed deadlines, and the doubtful signatures on the invoices.

I looked at the clock. I had a hearing in ten minutes with other parties and a full afternoon. I adjourned the hearing and announced I would inform Smith's Plumbing and Darlene Jones of my Judgment by mail. As I usually do when choosing this course of action, I told them I was certain they wanted me to consider all the evidence thoroughly so as to make an informed decision that was fair and just. Nobody ever has the temerity to disagree with that.

Privately, I was simply unable to make a decision on a moment's notice. I had some impressions about the various things I had heard, but no firm conclusion. I stacked the evidence up and left for chambers.

Once alone with the stack of photos and other papers, I looked again at the signatures on the various invoices, and realized that Darlene Jones's final swipe at Sam Smith about these signatures might well be the only thing at all that mattered about this case. I took the invoices home with me securely to study and ponder over.

Late into the night I examined the signatures with magnifying glasses and used various techniques to compare them, superimposing this one over that. I finally arrived at some definite conclusions, emailed myself at work with my notes so I could access them at chambers in the morning, and then went to bed.

The following Judgment went out by the U.S. Postal Service the next day:

THE JUDGMENT

The issues raised in court concerning quality of workmanship, deadlines and other matters all hinge upon the more fundamental issue of whether or not valid contracts exist between the parties. The Court therefore examined that issue first. If the alleged contracts do not qualify for the Court's enforcement, the Plaintiff's case fails.

Defendant's Exhibit 1 consists of two invoices that were part of the total job performed by Smith's Plumbing for Darlene Jones. They were not the subject of this suit by the Plaintiff. The invoices were submitted by Ms. Jones to show examples of her signature.

1. Plaintiff's Exhibit 1 consists of pink copies of two invoices, nos. 1234 and 1235. The signatures on the two invoices, which are for different items and are dated January 3 and January 6 of this year, respectively, appear even upon casual observation to be nearly identical. In her testimony, Jones drew the Court's attention to characteristics of the signatures that she said supported her contention that she did not make them.

    The signature on 1235 wavers along its path, showing what is commonly associated with a slow, deliberate inscription, such as is typical with tracing. The signature on 1234 also has indications of tracing. Overall, it is smoother than the signature on 1235, but it has a telltale slow-down in the upper loop of the capital D, and a smaller slow-down variation in the loop of the lower case L. Superimposing 1234 on 1235, the otherwise nearly identical nature of the two signatures becomes undeniably evident: they have the same slant; the signatures are on the baseline of the invoice in the same spot; and each initial capital slightly crosses the bottom line at the same point.

It is the finding of the Court upon the preponderance of the evidence in the record that the signatures on invoices 1234 and 1235 were duplicated from another source.

2. The signature on 1020, dated December 23 of last year, which Jones testifies is genuine, bears the same similarity to the signatures on 1234 and 1235 as those signatures have to each other. All three are in the same place on their respective invoices, have the same slant, and the same length. Their letters are in the same places and have the same size and shape.

Overlaying the genuine signature of 1020 on the other two, it is apparent that the signature on one of the copies of 1020, either the pink or the yellow—both of which Plaintiff possessed, was traced onto the other two invoices. The one distinct difference in the two copied signatures and the genuine one is in the ornate capital D of "Darlene". Close examination of the original shows that Jones's pen either lifted slightly from the paper or skipped in the rear curve of the letter. The copies, however, evince that the maker of the duplicate signatures mistook the open space as representing the ending and beginning of two line segments, as the copies are consistent with a pen or stylus being lifted and another line beginning a short distance away deliberately. This fact, too, weighs heavily in favor of the conclusion that the copies were made from the same source.

The Court finds that the genuine signature on invoice 1020 was the source for the signatures on both 1234 and 1235. The signatures on these two invoices were not made by Ms. Jones.

3. In considering the evidence of forgery, the Court noted with particular interest that after Jones asserted that the signatures on 1234 and 1235 were forgeries, Smith never contradicted that

testimony. He asked no questions in cross examination testing her evidence, and though he was given specific opportunity by the Court to offer rebuttal testimony, he said nothing about the signatures, even to deny that they were forged. Nevertheless, although the Court has found that they were forged, the Court has no indication of who is responsible for the traced signatures, nor enough evidence to indicate the precise purpose in forging them.

4.   In this civil matter, the critical issue for the Court is whether or not invoices 1234 or 1235 can be enforced. Since the Court finds that the signatures on these two invoices were forged, the Court must also find that the work orders/invoices are not valid contracts. This Court, therefore, will not enforce them.

Since the Plaintiff's entire claim rests on the enforcement of contracts created by the signatures on invoices 1234 and 1235, the Plaintiff's Complaint must therefore be dismissed and Judgment rendered wholly for the Defendant.

Counterclaim

In the matter of the Counterclaim, the Court disallowed Defendant's exhibit intending to establish by an unauthenticated estimate what her damages would be from hiring another party to complete work that Smith's Plumbing did not do. The Court does not need to determine either the issue of whether or not Jones's own dismissal of Smith's Plumbing from the job was in large part the reason for Plaintiff's inability to complete the work, or the issue of whether slow work unreasonably delayed completion. The mere fact that Jones was not able to show by admissible evidence that she had monetary damages leads the Court to dismiss the Counterclaim against Smith's Plumbing.

The claims of each party are therefore dismissed with no award made.

I have always wondered what the faces of parties look like when they read judgments received in their mail at home. I see their blank stares, glowering scowls, smirking smiles, tightly controlled anger or barely concealed delight when I deliver a judgment from the bench. I can only guess what sighs of relief, huffs of disgust, outbursts of obscenity or expressions of consternation take place thirty seconds after the envelope is opened.

The mystery will remain, I suppose.

15

For Love of a Harley

One of the staples of the Magistrate Court is the Claim and Delivery action. In my court, about half of these actions concern furniture or miscellaneous consumer electronics that have been offered as collateral on loans quickly defaulted on. Perhaps another ten percent deal with odd items left behind by departing lovers and others and then denied to them as a form of revenge. But the rest of these cases have to do with motor vehicles—the car somebody put up as security on a loan, the truck sold on owner financing that the purchaser didn't then fully pay for—and in the following case, a motorcycle that changed hands three times.

THE PLEADINGS

Buster Smith came to the court at his wit's end about his 1988 Harley Davidson motorcycle that had been taken from him the previous evening. He explained that he had been at a charity benefit with crowds of other bikers, when Scooter Jones came up to him along with a Littleton police officer. Jones waved a title to the motorcycle in his hand and said he had come to take possession of it.

The back story was that Buster had bought the bike from Mickey Brown. Brown had bought the bike from Jones in boxes and had reassembled it. Brown in turn sold it to Smith, who made full payments within five weeks, but then Brown didn't transfer the title to Smith. He kept putting him off, saying he would have it in a few weeks.

Then Scooter Jones appeared at the charity motorcycle rally waving his title, and now Smith was out one motorcycle, which happened to be his only transportation. Buster Smith wanted to know what he could do through the court. I gave him the forms for a Claim and Delivery, since what he really wanted was the bike, not money. He filed the papers and the suit was served in a few days.

Scooter Jones informed the Court that he certainly would be at the hearing but he gave no details by way of any sort of Answer.

A few days before the hearing, I got a letter from a Chris Johnson, an attorney in nearby Bigtown, saying he would be representing Smith.

THE EVIDENCE

The day set for trial, Buster Smith came with attorney Johnson. Johnson, a forty-ish man with shaved head and muscular appearance specialized, as I later learned, in motorcycle cases of all kinds.

On the other side of the aisle was Scooter Jones, who was unrepresented. As I entered the courtroom, the three had been talking, and Johnson promptly informed me that he believed they had come to a solution to the matter.

Johnson summed up the situation pretty much as I had gathered it solely from Buster Smith's filing. "What we have here, your honor, is a case where Mr. Jones sold a 1988 Harley to a Mr. Mickey Brown, who obviously is not here today. Brown was supposed to make payments to Jones, and at some point, he defaulted, owing about $3,500.00. Mr. Jones had not signed over the title. He kept trying to get Mr. Brown to finish paying him, but Brown kept putting him off."

"Shortly before Mickey Brown defaulted, he sold the bike to my client, Buster Smith. My client fully paid for the bike and has a bill of sale. He has owned the bike for a little more than a year."

Johnson gestured at Mr. Jones. "About a month ago, Mr. Jones here managed to find out who Mr. Brown had sold the Harley to, and he took possession of it with the help of a Littleton police officer. My client then filed a Claim and Delivery, and that brings us here today." I nodded at all this, and Johnson continued.

"Your honor, my client feels he has a legal right to the possession of the bike. He has a bill of sale. He bought the Harley in good faith on promise of delivery of title. Mr. Jones doesn't really want the bike; he wants the money that is still owed to him by the man in the middle of all this, Mickey Brown."

"So, your honor, I believe we've worked out a solution, and I'd like to read it into the record as a settlement and if it meets with your honor's approval, I'd move that your honor order it to be done."

"Mr. Johnson," I said, "The magistrate court is always interested in promoting settlement, so let's hear it."

"What I propose," said Johnson, "and what my client and Mr. Jones have agreed to, is that Wednesday of this week we will all meet at my offices and Mr. Jones will turn over possession of the Harley to my client, and that my client will pay Mr. Jones $3,500.00—$500.00 down and $200.00 per week. Mr. Jones will have his money and Mr. Smith will have his transportation back. And then we," he said motioning to his client Buster Smith, "will go after Mr. Brown for the damages."

I jotted down the particulars and nodded to Johnson: "That suits the Court if it suits you. Is that what you agree to, Mr. Jones?" Jones nodded. So did Smith. "Very well," I said. "Mr. Johnson, will you draw the order or stipulation of settlement and send it to me to sign right away?"

"Yes, your honor," said Johnson, and the hearing was over. I remarked to the clerk on the way out that I was surprised that the matter had been settled so easily. I doubted I would have agreed to pay somebody else's debt on the prospect of suing him for it later. I expected to have a suit against Brown to come across my desk before too long.

POST HEARING

Of course, the matter was not over, not even between Smith and Jones.

First, I didn't get any copy of a settlement from Attorney Chris Johnson. But when the day Smith and Jones were to trade money for motorcycle came and went, I assumed all had gone as planned. In fact, two months passed and the case had been all but forgotten, when Buster Smith appeared at my office window and wanted to talk.

Buster Smith told me he went to Attorney Johnson's office, cash in hand on the day of the planned exchange, but Scooter Jones did not show up with the bike. Johnson called Jones. Jones said he didn't have the bike, that it was at another location, and he didn't have time to go get it and bring it back to meet Smith at Johnson's offices that day. He would have to postpone.

Smith was livid, and skeptical about Jones's truthfulness. In fact, in the next few weeks, as attorney Johnson tried again and again to contact Jones and arrange another meeting, Jones avoided calls, would not return calls when messages were left, and generally made it clear that he was thumbing his nose at the agreement he had made and at this Court, which had endorsed that agreement as its order.

Curiously, Buster Smith also intimated to me that his lawyer wasn't helping him. I gathered that Smith had made a pest of himself wanting Johnson to physically go force Jones to comply, and that Johnson had decided to drop him as a client. It may also have been, I thought, that Smith had not paid him anything.

I decided to write Mr. Johnson asking what the status of the case was, since his client had reappeared at the court and I felt that since he was the attorney of record for Mr. Smith, he should be doing the talking. That letter crossed paths in the mail with the order I had asked Johnson to produce two months before. He gave no indication in the short cover letter that there was anything amiss between him and his client.

From what Smith told me about Jones's not complying with the agreement made in court, I had just about decided to take Smith's request for the court to "do something!" as a Motion to Compel Settlement. But then Smith told me, "What I hear is that Scooter doesn't even have the bike anymore: he sold it." That changed everything. If it were true, then the only real course of action was to rule the parties back into court. I set a date, gave Smith verbal notice of it, and told him I would bring everyone back.

SECOND HEARING

After subpoenaing the parties and Mr. Johnson, as well as Mickey Brown and several other persons Smith said were involved, a hearing convened in a few days. I wanted to know why the order had not been complied with, and if I learned that Mr. Jones had no compelling reason for his failure, I intended to hold him in contempt. Depending on what transpired in this first stage of the hearing, I would go on to hear the original matter of the Claim and Delivery—no testimony had ever been taken on that complaint, as a settlement had been reached at the previous hearing.

I was robing up at the hour for the hearing when my clerk told me that the Defendant was not here yet. Smith and attorney Johnson were in the courtroom, as were all the other subpoenaed persons included the man in the middle of all this, Mickey Brown, but Jones was not there. I waited ten minutes and then entered the courtroom.

I noted first for the record that Jones was not present, I had the clerk to call his name at the courthouse door in compliance with the relevant statute, and then I ruled that the hearing would proceed in his absence and that he was at this point in default according to court rules.

"Let me see if I have the history of this case clear," I said to Mr. Johnson. I reviewed the facts as they had been stipulated at the previous hearing, meaning that Mr. Jones had agreed to the basic story. "And Mr. Brown didn't get title from Mr. Jones, which meant that he could not transfer title to Mr. Smith, is that correct?" I asked. Johnson said it was. A man in the courtroom identifying himself as Mickey Brown held up his hand to speak, but I didn't allow it.

Johnson apparently felt it was useful to add to his comments what I had been thinking for more than two months, now: "It appears, your honor, that there may be a question of charges for title fraud in the case of Mr. Brown." I looked back at Mr. Brown and saw that he looked a bit shaky.

I then asked Johnson to tell me what had taken place with the planned exchange, and his report was exactly what his client had given me. Neither Johnson nor Smith could say authoritatively that Jones had sold the Harley, but it was the information that they got "in the community"—meaning the biking community.

"Since Mr. Jones has not appeared today," I said, "he has made things easier for us. Since he is in default, I am going to proceed on the basis of Rule 11 of Magistrate Court Rules and grant the Plaintiff the relief asked in his original Complaint and Affidavit for Claim and Delivery."

I swore in Mr. Smith and asked him a few questions just to fill in any holes in the facts I needed to know for the sake of the Claim and Delivery action. Then I asked Mr. Johnson if he wanted to Move to Compel Settlement or go straight to a Claim and Delivery order. He opted to Compel Settlement.

"Then here's what we're going to do, Mr. Johnson," I said. "We're going to settle this thing today. I don't want to come back here for another hearing, and we won't need to. First, I'm going to grant the motion. I will issue an Order Compelling Settlement today, giving Mr. Jones ten days to comply with the settlement order. That's by the 4th of next month. If for any reason he does not comply—including the excuse that he doesn't have the bike anymore—then upon your affidavit returned to this court, I will hold Mr. Jones in contempt, and I will issue an Order of Dispossession for the Harley, and I'll send my Constable out to get it. If it can't be had—if, for instance, Mr. Jones has sold it as the word on the street has it—then I will give you, Mr. Smith, a Judgment for $7,500.00, the value of the Harley, as you have waived the amount over this Court's subject jurisdictional limit."

Smith nodded in satisfaction. Johnson said, "Thank you, your honor." But I wasn't finished.

"Mr. Brown," I said, looking back into the courtroom at Mickey, "You are not a party to the action here today, and though you were subpoenaed, your testimony was not needed since the Defendant did not show up. Neither is your name on any charging paper in a criminal matter. I do, however, have a word of warning for you."

"I am reminded of a verse from the Bible, Luke 12:58: "As you are going with your adversary to the magistrate, try hard to be reconciled on the way, or your adversary may drag you off to the judge, and the judge turn you over to the officer, and the officer throw you into prison." I peered at him for a second and then asked him, "Do you know what I'm telling you?"

Brown nodded slowly. I clarified the point so there would be no question: "Do your best to clear up these matters with all concerned, while you still can." Brown nodded again. I banged the gavel, and everybody rose to go.

ROUND THREE

In ten days, Buster Smith reappeared at the courthouse window. Attorney Johnson had arranged for Smith and Jones to meet at the police station next door to complete the exchange in fulfillment of the settlement. I directed Smith to the station entrance but before he left he expressed doubt that Jones would show and also complained that he was going to come out having spent far more on this Harley than he should have had to pay. He also believed that Jones was lying about not having been fully paid by Brown for the motorcycle. Smith was simply not a happy camper all around.

As it turned out, Jones did show up in a few minutes and made the exchange. The bike would not start. It had damaged parts from the seizure procedures performed when Jones took the bike from Smith at the charity rally. Smith estimated it would cost another $500.00 to fix it. I smothered an opinion that he should turn around and sue Jones for the cost—it simply wasn't my role.

Jones didn't bring a bill of sale to the exchange, but he was dutiful enough to go get one before the day was over, enabling Smith to get another temporary tag. Smith's lawyer, however, had neglected to include in the settlement an agreement that Jones would have himself shown as lienholder on the title and give it to Smith. That meant Smith's temporary tag, which he could get with the bill of sale alone, would run out in forty-five days, and he would be in the same fix as before—no title, no tag, and no legal riding.

I instructed Smith to update his lawyer. He said he was also going to talk about taking out a warrant for title fraud. Perhaps, he said, Mr. Brown, facing the prospect of even more criminal charges, would find a way to come up with the money that he owed somebody—either Jones, or now Smith—in exchange for dropped charges.

Smith dropped the matter of title fraud. And although he considered suing Jones for his other costs in the three months or so that Jones had possession of his only transportation, Smith finally decided to drop that matter as well. It wasn't the money. It was about the love of a Harley.

16

BE MINE

It doesn't take long for a magistrate to develop an immunity to shock. While there is apparently no end to the interesting predicaments people bring before the court, a judge realizes after a while that the unusual is the new normal. Nevertheless, what continues to be surprising is how pleadings and actual trial testimony tell stories that are sometimes night and day apart. An upcoming case may look like a routine variation on a common theme, but when testimony begins, a different story may emerge altogether.

Such was the case with a restraining order matter the Court heard. It sounded like the familiar, sad tale of a boyfriend-girlfriend breakup turned into a threatening situation.

THE PLEADINGS

Plaintiff Natalie Smith came to the Court to file for a Restraining Order against Marlin Jones. The Defendant lived in the Court's jurisdiction, but Smith lived two hours away. Smith's brief *ex parte* testimony for the Affidavit and Complaint for Restraining Order was that she and Jones had been boyfriend and girlfriend (they were both in their mid to late thirties) and that at some point she broke up with him. Jones did not take it well, said Smith, and she provided the Court with examples of text messages he had sent her in which he claimed that she belonged to him and threatened her with physical harm if she did not change her mind. Smith said she had found out that Jones had a criminal record and that she believed he meant what he said.

The Court found the evidence sufficient to issue a Temporary Restraining Order, and the action was served on Defendant Jones within a few days.

In restraining order actions, I may "tweak" the Summons to indicate that while the Defendant may wish to contest the action, he may on the other hand choose not to appear at the hearing and a one year Restraining Order will simply be issued. I have sometimes prevented a potentially violent standoff between warring parties by doing this. A Defendant may realize that the issuance of a Restraining Order is *almost* a foregone conclusion.

Nevertheless, this Court *never* reaches foregone conclusions. If defendants want to come to a hearing and testify, I will hear them, and sometimes the story they tell shatters the first impression left by plaintiffs. In this particular case, the Defendant didn't opt out of the hearing. He had something to say, and it was what both he and the Plaintiff said that provided the Court with a surprise.

THE EVIDENCE

The Court swore in Natalie Smith and asked her to tell what events led her to make her Affidavit and Complaint. Smith then filled in a blank the Court had no idea existed.

Plaintiff
"Mr. Jones and I met last year about Christmas on a BDSM website—for people with alternate lifestyles," she said. "I probably need to explain a bit." Actually, she didn't; my theoretical knowledge vastly exceeds my practical experience. I knew that BDSM was short for Bondage & Discipline, Dominance & Submission, Sadism and Masochism. The association most people make of this lifestyle with whips and such is grounded in actual practices of many BDSM "practitioners."

Natalie seemed just a bit amused by her own story, and I thought at first it was some embarrassment at having to tell the Court about her "alternate lifestyle." She said that during the latter part of the previous year she had decided to try something new and spice up her sex life by experimenting with BDSM. She liked being controlled when she had sex, so she found a BDSM website and joined to find a partner. Not long after, she had a contact from

Marlin. They met around Christmas at her home and spent a night together. They liked each other and decided to keep "hooking up." Natalie told the Court she was the submissive and Marlin was the dominant. In her words, these were "roles they played" as they pursued their sexual encounters. She played the role of slave and he was the master.

Jones was making noises from his table, little explosions of laughter that were barely muffled expressions of disbelief, presumably about the way Smith was spinning the story. The Court forbore and soon Jones brought himself under control.

Ms. Smith then said that a few months later she realized that Mr. Jones was becoming possessive and mean. After a particularly tense weekend together, she broke up with him by phone text message. Immediately afterward she said he called her and demanded that she reverse her decision. He warned her that she didn't have a right to drop him "just like that" and he said that she belonged to him. Two days later, he sent several text messages, the ones the Court had in pleadings already and that had provided the Court's justification for the Temporary Order. The messages began to look just a bit different in the light of Smith's unabashed testimony that Jones and she were in a dominant-submissive relationship.

Plaintiff Smith said she believed Jones's text threat, "You will meet Ur makr," because she found out that Jones had served time for attempted murder—eight years on a sentence of fifteen. She said that he hadn't told her this himself, but that she found it out from a friend.

On hearing this testimony, the court clerk hurriedly jotted a note and passed it over the side rail of the bench to me. "Do you have your gun," it said, and I said, "Yes, thank you, madam clerk." In fact, often I am armed in the courtroom, as judges with concealed weapons permits are specifically authorized to be. Considering the fact that I have no bailiff or any other person to act as security in my courtroom, a Bulldog .44 is often on my side at the ready should I need it, and of course I hope I never do.

Smith had no more to offer and the Court turned to Jones for any questions. Jones asked Smith if it weren't true that he had told her two days after they first met in person that he had a criminal past. She paused and then denied it. He asked if she had a background check run on him just after they met online. She admitted that she had asked a friend to run a background check but said it was more than a month later. Wasn't it true, he said, that she knew from the beginning that he had a record? She said, though unconvincingly, that she didn't. Jones appeared satisfied that he had demonstrated to the Court through several simple questions that he had disclosed his past in the interest of transparency. He didn't have any more questions.

Defendant

Smith was finished and the Court swore in Jones. Natalie Smith had painted Marlin Jones as villainous, but Jones didn't quite match up to the caricature, even though he did not deny his criminal record and didn't apologize for being involved in the BDSM lifestyle. He began by testifying that he never hid his past from anyone; he wasn't proud of his criminal record, but he had changed. Yes, he and Smith had met on the internet website, and he had told her where he lived so she could check him out and feel more confident about him. He pointed out to the Court very quickly that dominant-submissive relationships were *not role playing* but very serious life-roles that covered an entire relationship, both private and public.

Jones said that Smith had called him "My King," or just "King" from the start, and that he had always referred to her as "Princess." Jones testified that he believed Smith was taking the relationship seriously because they discussed her having herself tattooed with symbols of his ownership, and she had agreed. Jones submitted into evidence a print of a digital picture he had taken of a tattoo of a bar code registered to him and showing his ownership of Smith, with "My King" above the code and "Princess" below it. The tattoo was on her right buttock. The Court was thankful to have only verbal evidence of this fact.

Jones said that a few months ago Smith had suddenly begun

referring to him by his actual first name. That alarmed him, he said, because it strongly suggested that she was changing her approach to the relationship. When he brought up the subject at his house, it touched off an argument that resulted in her leaving suddenly and texting him that the relationship was over, just as Natalie had said she had done.

Jones explained to the Court that in a dominant-submissive lifestyle there is an accepted protocol for ending a relationship and that it requires that the dominant person "release" the submissive publicly. After their phone conversation in which they argued about Smith's desire to break up, Jones said he texted her in typical language for a dominant, and that a printout of the text exchange that Smith had submitted into pleadings should be clearly seen to be a dominant speaking in a commanding way to a submissive, attempting to discipline her.

The Court perused the text exchanges, which I had already begun to realize were more clearly explained as having reflected this "alternate lifestyle." Less and less did the exchange look like an actual and credible threat to kill Smith.

When Jones realized that Smith was adamant about breaking up, he released her and made the appropriate announcement to the BDSM community through the website.

Jones was finished testifying. I had thought of a few questions for each of them. I asked Smith if she hadn't testified earlier that after the text exchange in which she said Jones threatened to kill her, he had in fact not contacted her again. She confirmed that was so. And did she file for the Restraining Order two days *after* that text exchange. Yes. Was this the first such relationship she had ever been in? Yes. Was her joining the BDSM website the first time she had made a foray into this alternate lifestyle? Yes. Had she ever met and formed a relationship with anyone online before? No. She added that she had only been trying to "do something different to spice things up."

I asked Jones if he had been a dominant in a relationship before, and he said that he had. This was a confirmed and longtime style of life for him.

Neither party had any further testimony. I had been making notes during the entire proceeding and was ready to render a decision without further deliberation:

THE JUDGMENT

There is a growing body of cases dealing with the nature of dominant-submissive relationships as relates to possible criminal issues of assault and domestic abuse. The question courts find themselves addressing is whether or not permission has been given and acknowledged that some behavior that might otherwise be interpreted by a reasonable person as criminal, is in fact freely invited and is not otherwise criminal as long as it is consensual.

1. In this case, it appears to the Court on the preponderance of the evidence that the Defendant's actions or words were expressive of the role he was fulfilling in the relationship, a role that the Plaintiff had accepted and agreed to. It also appears certain to the Court that while the Defendant was engaged in a "life role" with the Plaintiff, the Plaintiff believed herself to be merely "*role playing*" with the Defendant, a fact that convinces the Court that the two had decidedly different sets of expectations.
2. These different expectations eventually produced conflict when Smith began to imply she wanted the relationship to transition into something more toward the societal norm and probably permanent. Jones recognized that change and it upset him, leading to the disagreement, but the entire unpleasantness lasted only a few days. By then, as the evidence *from both sides* clearly shows, Jones realized it was time to call it quits, and he did. In fact, he abruptly ceased his demands of Smith when he saw that the terms of the relationship had changed. In this, his actions showed integrity on his part, as he realized that his dominant behavior was no longer consensual.
3. The testimony of both parties establishes a wholly different

relationship between Plaintiff and Defendant than the Court was led to believe existed by virtue of the Plaintiff's *ex parte* testimony alone. In the light of the dominant-submissive nature of the relationship, the Court finds that the Defendant's phone demands and text messages were delivered in the context of his role as the master and hers as the slave. Consequently, the preponderance of the evidence does not uphold a finding that Defendant's texts were criminally threatening, and the Court believes that the Plaintiff had sufficient history with the Defendant by this time that she should have realized this fact.

4. **Law:** A Restraining Order may be granted upon a finding of harassment or stalking. The law defines harassment as:

> "...a pattern of intentional, substantial, and unreasonable intrusion into the private life of a targeted person that serves no legitimate purpose and causes the person and would cause a reasonable person in his position to suffer mental or emotional distress."

5. The Court finds first that a pattern was not established. While two events *may* constitute a pattern, it appears that the phone call and the texting event did not by themselves establish a pattern in this case. Neither can the Court find that the contacts were unreasonable or had no legitimate purpose, their being occasioned by a breakup, which in and of itself is a serious interpersonal issue that almost always prompts reasonable attempts by one person to try to change the other person's mind and heart. Thus, the contacts had a legitimate purpose.

6. By definition, then, the Court has declined to find grounds for granting this Restraining Order. Since the parties have been involved with each other previously and the present trouble is due to an unpleasant breakup, I grant myself judicial privilege in advising both of you to stay clear of each other and to

consider your relationship over entirely. Once facing off in court as you have today, further involvement might escalate to criminal conduct, and I do not wish to see you here on such matters.

However, because the evidence does not lead even by a simple preponderance to a finding of harassment by the Defendant, the Court renders Judgment for the Defendant and dismisses the Complaint.

I watched the parties as the hearing concluded. The Defendant left the courtroom looking satisfied in victory. Curiously, however, I noted that the Plaintiff still wore the slight smile that she had frequently displayed throughout the hearing, though now it didn't suggest embarrassment. Nor did she appear the slightest bit upset as she dug into her purse to pay the deferred filing fee for the action she had just lost. In fact, she seemed to be in quite a good mood.

I could only conclude that she was happy to have gotten whipped in court.

17

I Don't Want You Anymore

Among situations evoking the greatest sadness in a judge's heart are those family relationships that should be marked by caring and compassion but that have degenerated into hostility and contempt. Obviously, divorce courts deal with such situations every day, but even more heart-wrenching, in my opinion, is the loss of natural affection between brothers, sisters, or a parent and child. Such was the case with a mother and daughter who found themselves before me in an eviction hearing.

The Pleadings

Sarah Smith, a woman of about sixty, filed for eviction against her daughter Jenna Jones, a woman of about thirty-five, who paid rent and lived in the same house with her mother on Pleasant Oak Street. On the Application for Eviction form, the mother checked the box labeled "Tenant has violated terms of the lease as follows:" and then she wrote in the blank, "She needs medical/psychiatric help which she refuses to do and I cannot care for her medical/personal needs at this time."

The clerk had spoken with Mrs. Smith when she filed the case and knew that the defendant/tenant was her daughter. I opined to the clerk that if the lease—if in fact there were one—did not specifically provide that Ms. Jones had to take medicine or go to a doctor, Smith may have filed with an inadequate reason to evict.

Jones responded to the ten-day Notice to Show Cause by telephoning the court and asking for a hearing. (Jenna Jones was really Jenna Smith, unmarried, but because all defendants in this book are "Jones," I am referring to her as Jones rather than Smith, just to keep the parties straight.) The court clerk had great difficulty understanding Jenna Jones, who spoke with slurred speech and defective enunciation. In the course of conversation and later contacts she gathered that Ms. Jones had multiple sclerosis and was always in her bed or in a wheelchair. The clerk told me I might need an interpreter of sorts simply to understand Ms. Jones. A day later, after confirming a hearing date with all parties, the clerk told me that Ms. Jones would be brought to the courthouse by a medical transport team and would be brought into the court strapped onto a gurney to give her defense.

The Evidence

In the courtroom the day of the hearing, the Plaintiff sat at her table alone, tired and haggard looking. Behind her were some friends of the Defendant and Defendant's brother, who as it turned out lived in the same house. Behind Defendant Jones was the transport team in their uniforms. Defendant Jenna Jones lay strapped to the transport gurney, which was raised slightly on the head end so that she could see better. Beside Jones was another woman who turned out to be a social worker who visited in the home once a week and was very familiar with Jones. Once or twice she helped the Court clarify something Jones said in testimony.

Plaintiff

Mrs. Smith told a brief tale in an almost exhausted manner of how her daughter had come to live with her after spending some years in New Jersey with her other daughter. Smith never explained Jenna's condition or even referred to it other than to say that Jenna needed help and wouldn't get it. I listened to her briefly describe her complaint, asked a few questions, and then heard from the Defendant as well, before I was able to piece together the story.

Jones had gone to live with her sister about a decade before. The reason she left there after about eight years was unclear. Jones's support came from Social Security. A personal representative managed Jones's financial matters and wrote a check to the care giver with whom Jones lived, whomever that might be. For eight years, that had been her sister. When Jones moved down to live with her mother, the checks began coming to her mother. She received about $900.00 per month.

Finding out that Social Security was involved, the Court wanted to make certain that the living arrangement between Smith and Jones did not involve some Federal or State agency that would either take this matter out of the Magistrate Court or involve housing laws that might have an impact on the eviction. The Court asked multiple questions to determine this matter and was finally satisfied that there were no contracts with a government entity. Smith got the money and used some of it to buy food and other items for Jones, so there was more to the money than simply rent. Daughter Jones was paying mother Smith to take care of her. Smith had finally decided that she simply wasn't able to do so.

Smith said the problem was that Jones kept her up all hours of the night, shouted, and was belligerent. Smith said, "She called the police on me." She did not add what reason Jones may have had to call police to the home.

I wanted to know what the rental situation was, if there were a lease, how much Jones paid, etc. There was no written lease, said Smith, only an agreement that Jones could live there "month to month," and that the Social Security money would come to Smith in order to cover rent and whatever care she provided. The Court asked Smith to repeat and make abundantly clear whether there were any term of tenancy longer than month to month. No, there wasn't.

Before asking if Jones had any questions, I asked Smith again to tell me if, when Jones had come back to live with her, there were any conversation and agreement about Jones's medical care or medicine. No, there wasn't.

Sarah Smith was dabbing at her eyes and fighting back tears. It was unclear to me whether her tears reflected a broken heart or something less expressive of love for her daughter. I believed the latter, but I could not imagine being in her shoes and feeling that for my own sanity I would have to evict my own daughter. Then again, it wasn't the first eviction or summary ejectment of close family members I had dealt with. I averaged one every two months or so.

Defendant Jones, on the other hand, seemed eager to give her defense and not at all hopeless as her mother seemed. I swore her in, not considering before routinely instructing her to raise her right hand that she might have difficulty doing it. She did, but only slightly, and she took the oath.

Defendant

Jenna Jones confirmed the basic facts that her living arrangement with her mother was a month to month tenancy. Her account immediately introduced the involvement of her brother, however, who kept her up late at night she said, made coffee at 3 a.m. and argued with her. The circumstances revolving around the call to the police were never made clear by either Smith or Jones, but from what the Court gathered from Jones, her mother had threatened her in some way. Smith never disputed this testimony or anything Jones said, and the Court gave both parties ample opportunity for rebuttal testimony.

I had no real difficulty making out what Jones was saying, as long as I could see her lips. She became a bit animated when referring to her mother at one point, and she hoisted her shoulders up a few inches to turn her head toward Smith when she spoke with frustration about how her mother was impatient with her. It was clear to the Court that Jones was not a sedate person by nature, but it was also clear that mother and daughter didn't get along well and that probably each of them was responsible for generating disagreement and contention in the home.

Throughout the hearing, I had used my pastoral counseling voice and leaned forward, smiling slightly as I spoke to each party. I was cognizant of the possibility of being thought biased by either side: by Smith if I acted overly sympathetic toward Jones because of her physical condition; or by Jones if I heard the case perfunctorily and rubber stamped the eviction without considering Jones's story. I had treated both of them with gentleness and respect, wanting to create a sense of the Court's empathy with both sides. When they were both finished, I had no need to deliberate in chambers. The solution was obvious.

THE JUDGMENT

To the weary mother and waiting daughter I wore a fatherly, furrowed brow of compassion and concern, and spoke off the cuff and from the heart:

Mrs. Smith, when you first applied for this eviction, I assumed I would have to look for some provision in a lease that your daughter might have violated. I find, however, that there is no lease, as the two of you agree, and that the two of you are bound only by the provisions of the Landlord-Tenant Law of this State. That law states in part that a tenant must "conduct himself... in a manner that will not disturb other tenants' peaceful enjoyment of the premises." I have listened to your stories and asked you numerous questions and while it appears that there is discord between you and even incidents of arguing, it doesn't appear that Jenna has violated the provisions of the law. Even if she had failed to act in accord with the tenant obligation I just quoted from the law, you would be obligated to give her a fourteen-day notice with the right to cure—to fix what was wrong—before you could evict. I heard nothing about that kind of warning.

In addition, it is clear to me that this is a unique situation. Jenna is not merely a roomer in your house. She has access to any part of it and is after all your daughter. Had you had no rental agreement, you might have demanded that she leave summarily, and if she didn't, you could have filed for Summary Ejectment of Trespasser, but those were not the circumstances. Furthermore, the situation is made more complicated by the presence of the brother, who appears to the Court to have been a provocateur.

I would not do substantial justice if I approved your application for ejectment on the grounds you have specified, as supported by the evidence you offer. I find that the Defendant, your daughter, has not violated a provision of the Landlord-Tenant law justifying her ouster. For that reason, I must deny your request of the Court.

You know, and I believe that Jenna is aware of this as well, that in a month-to-month tenancy, you do not have to have grounds to end the tenancy when you like. You only have to give a thirty-day notice of the end of tenancy, and the tenant must vacate or be subject to eviction. Now, I am not recommending that you do such. I am merely advising you of the law and the services of the court. In fact, I would hope that you and your daughter could pass this episode and move into a better time of life. That, however, is not in my power to order or bring about, though I wish it were.

Judgment is for the Defendant. I wish you both well.

I believed that my decision would accomplish four things. First, strictly speaking, it accomplished substantial justice, given the particulars of the case. Second, since the hearing took place on the 14th of the month, it gave Jenna Jones about six weeks to find another place to live if her mother decided to give her a thirty-day notice of end of tenancy on the 1st of the following month. Third, my decision assured Plaintiff Sarah Smith that although she lost her eviction case on the present grounds, she could still evict her daughter if she insisted on doing so, within six weeks or perhaps eight, by filing a sure-fire eviction action if Jenna did not move out after a thirty-day notice. And fourth, my decision made it possible, just possible, for mother and daughter to go home, cry together, apologize for their attitudes towards each other, and make a new start.

It probably wasn't going to happen, but it was the best I could do for all parties, where the love of a mother and daughter was just a memory of those first precious years when both were bonded by the warm heart of nature.

As the transport team readied the gurney to go and my robes swished through the rear door of the courtroom, I heard the slight struggle of Jenna Jones's voice as she called out, "Thank you, your honor."

18
BLACK JACK, TRADE BACK

In a playground game of tag, quickly saying "Blackjack, no tradebacks" or "Jack Jack," or "tagbacks," or some other variant, disallows a tagged child from returning the tag immediately. It's an informal rule children generally honor. In court, however, there is no such rule. Jack may trade back freely.

Occasionally a person comes to court seeking to be paid and instead goes away owing money. One circumstance in which this tends to take place is when a plaintiff files suit in an attempt to make a preemptive strike in the midst of a controversy, but the strategy backfires: instead of merely defending himself, the defendant countersues; the court is not snowed by the plaintiff's aggressive offensive maneuver; and the true facts tell a story at dipolar opposites from the plaintiff's original allegations.

THE PLEADINGS

Plaintiff Beth Smith filed suit against Marty Jones, her landlord, for damages to her car from a garage door, for the cost of mold testing, and for return of her prepaid rent on a house Jones leased to her ten months previously. Smith alleged she and her fifteen-year-old son had become sick from mold in the house. She listed numerous safety issues she had discovered in the home, including a tree hanging over the master bedroom that she feared would fall—the thought of which kept her up nights. She sought to recover a total of more than $8,000.00 in damages.

Upon being served, Defendant Jones acquired counsel and submitted an Answer and Counterclaim. He denied every allegation and asked the Court instead to award him an amount to be proven at trial for damages to the home. He also requested that the Court order that he could retain the prepaid rent as damages for the Plaintiff's abandonment of the premises, and that the

Court further order Plaintiff to pay an additional six months of unpaid rent as lost rent under the eighteen-month lease.

The Evidence

A hearing was scheduled for a day about two months after the Plaintiff filed. As the day arrived I wondered if the hour and a half allotted for the trial would even be necessary, because of the issue of whether or not the Magistrate Court had jurisdiction over the matter. Normally, this question is determined before the suit is even accepted for filing, but in this instance the matter was unclear. Plaintiff's claim was for more than the usual jurisdictional limit of the Magistrate. Our state law gives the Magistrate Court concurrent jurisdiction with Circuit Courts "in all matters between landlord and tenant," which means that in landlord-tenant matters, there is no dollar limit to the amount of relief either one may seek and be awarded. The key issue, however, is whether the landlord or the tenant, whichever is the complainant, files the suit while the tenant is in possession of the land. In this case, in other words, was the tenant really a tenant when she filed the suit?

From the pleadings, it was not clear whether or not the Plaintiff was in possession of the property at the time she filed. She didn't state such a fact anywhere in her Complaint or in subsequent documents she filed, and Defendant's Answer stated that Smith had abandoned the property, but it gave no date she did so.

A few concise questions at the beginning of the hearing established to my satisfaction that the Plaintiff was still a tenant when she filed suit. She left the property very shortly thereafter. Defendant's Answer and Counterclaim was filed after Plaintiff moved out of the property, and the Counterclaim turned out to be for even more than the Plaintiff's suit, but the Plaintiff's filing while still in possession settled the issue: jurisdiction was proper for the Magistrate. I settled into my chair and anticipated we would be in the courtroom for an hour or more.

Plaintiff

Beth Smith began by describing how she, on the heels of a terrible divorce, had been forced to look for a new home and had found the Jones property through a local real estate agent. The monthly rent was $1,850.00. She said she had to go about everything in haste and didn't realize until she had been in the house for a while that it had lots of safety issues, including mold, which she said had made her and her son "very sick." She wasn't aware, she said sarcastically, that she needed to be a professional building inspector to see problems in a house.

Smith had come prepared with forty or more photographs of the inside of the house she rented from Marty Jones. She began with these pictures, extremely amateurish photos often out of focus or framed in such a way that they were difficult to orient or made it difficult for the viewer to locate the scenes depicted in the house. She quickly flipped through images she said were mold here and there along baseboards or in tile grout, around window casings or along caulk.

Some photos depicted water stains. Smith said these stains were caused by water leaks, one of which came from the upstairs toilet. She described flushing the toilet one day when it "sprayed water all over." She made a gesture that looked like a fountain gushing upward. The description was curious for a home toilet, and the Court asked several questions about it—was the toilet a high pressure valve type, as in commercial restrooms, or a pressure-assist type? —etc. She put on a confused look and tried using other descriptions. Her son, sitting near her, whispered to her to say that the toilet "overflowed," and she repeated this description. I was having difficulty imagining that she had never seen a toilet overflow and didn't know to describe it that way. Was she playing dumb? She said she didn't know she could turn off the "little things in the back," meaning apparently the supply lines to the toilet, so the water continued to overflow and eventually it seeped through the floor and damaged the ceiling below, which was in the kitchen.

Smith described how she called Jones about the toilet and that he came, and he said the toilet was operating correctly. His assessment was that Smith's son had plugged the toilet with excess tissue or was otherwise responsible. Smith ridiculed Jones's pronouncement of the toilet's proper operating condition and added some remarks intended to characterize Jones as an inattentive landlord on other occasions when she called him. Then she added another reminder of how she was going through such a difficult time with the divorce and needed someone to help her.

Plaintiff Smith then pulled a sheaf of documents from a file folder and said she wanted to show the Court the results of a mold test she had done. I had already seen a mold test submitted into pleadings, and though I had not evaluated it fully, I had noted that the report at least appeared to have been done in a decidedly non-professional way. I also saw that there did not appear to be anyone in the courtroom who was there to testify for Mrs. Smith as to the mold report, which meant that the report would be inadmissible hearsay.

No sooner had Smith held up the paper and said, "Here is a mold report," than Xena Williams, Defendant Jones's attorney, rose: "Objection, your honor: hearsay." I asked if Mrs. Smith had a witness from the inspection company to authenticate the report. No. I disallowed the report.

"Well," she said, "They couldn't come because this thing was rescheduled three times by your people and they finally just refused to come." Smith was blaming the court staff for her lack of witnesses. I asked, "Did you subpoena the witness?" She hadn't. I consulted the case file and saw also that the hearing had been continued only once. In fact, I remembered the reason, which was that attorney Williams's daughter had emergency surgery the day of the originally scheduled trial. Finally, I reminded Smith that in the instructions she was sent about the day of trial, she was told that she needed "live witnesses, not letters or statements from persons who were not in court." Unable to answer these facts, she offered no other defense of her unpreparedness.

Smith seemed initially stymied a bit by the ruling, but she had another paper she then found and held up, saying she wanted to show me a letter from a doctor—

"Objection," said Williams, "Hearsay."

"Mrs. Smith, is the doctor here?" I asked. He wasn't, and Smith didn't seem to understand why he needed to be. Apparently the lesson taught one minute ago had not thoroughly sunk in. I disallowed the doctor's letter, explaining that the other side could not cross examine a letter.

"Well," she said, almost muttering, "my son and I were very sick from all that mold." Williams objected to the continued reference to mold now that the mold report had been disallowed. I sustained the objection, but both Williams and I knew that Smith would find it impossible to call whatever it was she thought was mold, something else.

I looked at the boy next to Beth Smith, as I had from time to time, and thought I discerned something other than a confirmation of what his mother was saying. He seemed almost imperceptibly embarrassed by her story.

Smith moved on. She began to describe one morning she was headed to work, backed out of the garage, and suddenly the garage door "just fell down on my car." She produced photos of the back of the car, which the Court initially had difficulty recognizing as such. Finally, it appeared that the pictures were of the trunk of a car and a scratch extending from the horizontal surface near the back of the trunk and over the curve, going down toward the latch and the bumper. She said the door stuck on her car and wouldn't let go.

Smith called Jones right away. Jones said he was on his way out of town for a vacation and couldn't see to the door for two weeks. Knowing, or believing at least, that she couldn't call a garage door company in an emergency, Smith said she took the door down herself to get it off her car. The inconsistency of this testimony with what Smith had already said about her generally helpless state and her lack of mechanical knowledge, led the Court to raise an eyebrow. I'm not certain I would know myself where to start trying to disassemble and take off a double-wide garage door. Somehow, however, Mrs. Smith did so and left the pieces in the driveway. (I suspected the son was involved and maybe a neighbor.)

In a few weeks, Smith filed suit over damages to her car, which had been repaired at the surprisingly low cost of $180.00, and she threw in the complaints about mold. She wanted her prepaid rent back for the months left on the lease. She started looking for another place to live. She didn't need this sort of difficulty. After all, did the Court remember, she had just been through a messy divorce? And of course, there was the mold, and they were sick—

"Objection."

"Sustained."

With a sort of huff and sniff, Smith sat back, and I asked if she was ready for any questions the Defense might have. She was.

Xena Williams asked the Court for permission to call a witness out of order, because he needed to leave and she anticipated a very lengthy cross examination before we would even get to the presentation of the defense. I looked at the clock. The hour I thought we would be there had already passed. The parties for the next case had come into the back of the courtroom. I okayed the exception, and Williams called Paul Green, a garage door technician.

After Williams asked him several questions about his work, his experience and his training, she asked him specifically about his service call to the house in question in this case. Green testified that he had been called to the property after Smith moved out, when Jones returned from his trip, found Smith gone, and found the garage door in pieces in the driveway. Green was qualified as an expert in his field, and Williams asked him for his opinion about several issues. Essentially, Green said that from the marks on the door, the condition of the frame, bent pieces and other facts, his opinion was that Smith had begun backing out of the garage before the door had gone up completely and that she had run into it.

Smith cross examined and demanded to know if Green had been there. Had he seen her leave for work the day of the incident? Obviously, he hadn't. Then how could he say what happened? She looked at me and complained. "Can he just guess like that?"

I took a moment, as I often do, to educate the party on some procedure in court. Williams had asked questions designed to establish that Green was an expert in his field, and though she had not actually asked that the Court qualify him as an expert witness, I had done so, and I had allowed him therefore to give his opinion. That was why he could say what he did. He added that he had seen hundreds of garage doors damaged by cars, and that he had no doubt about his professional opinion in this case.

Not satisfied, but silenced anyway, Smith sat down. She had no more questions of Green. I dismissed Green and he left the courtroom.

It was now time for Williams to cross examine Smith. She began with the lease, going through it meticulously and asking Smith if she had agreed to its terms—to maintain the property, to refrain from making improvements or taking out or putting in fixtures, appliances, etc. without the landlord's permission. Yes, she had agreed to those things. Had she agreed to the addenda, one of which obligated her to pay attorney fees for the landlord if he had to bring suit to enforce the terms of the lease. Smith said yes, she had agreed to that provision, too.

Williams was done quickly with cross examining Smith. She had simply set her up for the coming presentation of Defendant's counterclaim, and she didn't intend to present a defense if she could avoid it. I asked if Smith had more witnesses and she didn't. I then turned to Williams for the Defense, and she made the somewhat typical motion for a directed verdict, arguing that Smith had not presented evidence sufficient for the Court to render judgment for her.

Normally, I deny motions for directed verdicts, although I always give them some thought. In fact, long before a plaintiff rests, usually I'm thinking about whether I might consider a directed verdict. In this case, I had come into the hearing expecting the Plaintiff to follow up on her many documents and statements in pleadings by giving a thorough and convincing case that she had been taken advantage of by a lazy and inattentive landlord and that she deserved relief. Instead, from the start she had appeared to be presenting a melodrama to play on the Court's sympathy, and she had schlepped through her testimony attempting to pawn off baseless accusations, half-baked opinions, generalizations and illogical conclusions—as well as inadmissible out-of-court statements—as solid evidence of her claims. I could see no reason the Defendant had to present a defense at all.

After asking Smith if she had any argument against the motion for a directed verdict, and having to explain what one was, she said she didn't guess so. Clearly she didn't know how to respond.

Still, I presented my ruling as gently as possible. I think she was expecting it by this point.

> Plaintiff has failed to meet her burden to convince me by a preponderance of evidence of the factuality of her claims or that her request for relief is warranted. Even without the Defendant's presentation of a defense, the case fails on the merits, I said. The motion for directed verdict is granted. The Complaint is dismissed.

"Ms. Williams," I said, "are you ready to present evidence on the Counterclaim?" She was.

Defense

Williams began by calling Defendant Marty Jones to the stand and asking him some questions about how he came to rent the house in question to Beth Smith. Jones said it was nothing unusual; his realtor told him someone wanted to view the house. When it came to talking about terms, he found out, because Smith told him, that she had been through a terrible divorce and that for a reason not explained she had terrible credit. Smith, however, offered to pay him a year's rent up front, and Jones agreed to the lease.

Moving on to other subjects, Xena Williams began questioning Jones about the house itself. Williams had been in my court two years or so earlier and had been wowed by the technological wizardry in the facility. The court building belongs to the city. My county court rents space from the city and shares the courtroom. The appointments and electronic gadgets in the state-of-the-art courtroom exceed those of even the Circuit Courts in our county. Williams had come prepared for this hearing with a PowerPoint™ presentation. She had plugged her laptop computer into the receptacle on the defense table and now displayed the presentation on the two large, 52" monitors to either side of the courtroom as well as the monitors on each table and the one on my bench. She asked Marty Jones to go through this presentation of photographs with her, a series of before-and-after views of the outside and inside of the home.

The presentation itself was very basic, but the impression it began to leave immediately was powerful. The house, far from being an average dwelling in a state of some disrepair, as the Plaintiff had implied it was, was an impressive, 3,000 sq. ft. edifice in very good condition when the Plaintiff-tenant had taken possession. Room to room, the presentation's before-pictures showed a house that was well painted, clean, nicely appointed, and in excellent condition throughout. The after-pictures, however, were another story.

Plaintiff had left the house with large, overly patched nail holes and other imperfections, dozens of them in every room. She had failed to clean adequately and there were many corners and crevices where various kinds of dirt and stains had accumulated. She had not maintained the gutters, and they had stopped up and allowed water to flow behind the fascia board and cause leaks and stains various places. She had broken a few doors and torn several window screens. She had possibly painted upstairs windows shut. And in moving out, she or moving men had dragged furniture down the steps leaving ground-in grime that probably would not be able to be removed.

Mr. Jones testified from a background of construction and home renovation. He gave costs for replacement, repair and painting as he went along, in response to Williams' plodding questions. Smith became agitated and objected at one point—to what, I could not at first tell.

"This is so repetitive," she complained. "She keeps saying the same thing." Williams had been using stock legal phrases about each detailed element of her questioning—"Does this picture fairly and accurately represent—" etc.

"Unless you have an objection to the relevance of the testimony," I said, "I'm going to overrule. Of course, you should be keeping notes about what you'd like to ask the witness in cross examination." I like to be helpful and never to come off as scolding a party, even one who was becoming increasingly tedious.

Williams continued her questioning. The pictures showed room after room where it was apparent that Smith had taken down the light fixtures and ceiling fans and replaced them with others. Most, though not all of these fixtures were found upstairs in the bonus room. Several were simply missing. Smith had taken down her fixtures when she left but had not replaced the original ones. The lease prohibited her having done any of it.

[I inferred from the ongoing evidence that Smith had not done any of this work herself but that she had paid people to install the fixtures. The growing impression I had was that Smith had plenty of money, but not as much good sense.]

The photos showed that Smith had damaged blinds, chipped woodwork and nicked walls. In a few places where she had done some sort of wall repair, possibly long before the events that led to her moving out, she had done an uneven job of spackling and had painted with a close-but-no-cigar color of paint.

When Williams had finished with her witness, I asked Smith if she had any questions for him. She asked the Defendant if he hadn't in fact given her permission to install other light fixtures. He looked her squarely in the eye and said he had not. She looked at me and back at Jones, and with just a bit too much drama she asked if Jones knew he was under oath. Jones didn't flinch. "I never gave you permission," he said.

My immediate thought was that I needed to assess the moment and decide whether or not I believed that Jones was telling the truth. Nothing about his testimony so far suggested that he was prevaricating in any way. On the other hand, increasing indications came from Smith that she was spinning a tale. Whatever back story there was to this matter, I believed that Smith was trying to get the Court to believe she had permission to alter the premises, when the opposite was almost certainly true.

Finally, Williams asked Jones about the lease, the Plaintiff's abandonment of the premises, and how many months rent she had already paid. Smith had abandoned the property about June 15 of the present year, having three more months of rent already paid and six more months of her lease for which she would owe rent as it came due on the 1st of each month. Landlord Jones had been occupied with repairs for two months since the abandonment and had now entered a listing agreement with a realtor. He was asking the Court to be able to retain all the prepaid rent and to recover the next six months of rent as damages for the abandonment. He had changed the locks on the house in June and had begun his inspection and repair after documenting everything for the litigation.

Smith had no more questions and I dismissed Jones. Attorney Williams called Larry Brown to the stand, who turned out to be a mold inspector. Defendant had engaged his own expert after Smith moved out, and Larry Brown had done a thorough and professional inspection. Williams moved into evidence the report and the analysis, which Brown explained. The house had no mold problem. There was evidence in two places that there had been some active mold perhaps years ago, but there was no test showing any active mold growth anywhere in the dwelling.

Smith had no questions. She acted as if the whole proceeding at this point were rigged against her.

Williams appeared to be resting her case. I asked her to give me the bottom line of the Defendant's damages. She added up the figures and said, "$21,880.00."

I asked Williams to close, and she did so in a couple of sentences—refreshing economy for such a long presentation. I then asked Smith if she wanted to offer a summary statement, explaining that it was simply her way of telling me what she believed the evidence had showed me.

Smith was sullen. "All I can say is they lied. They all lied." And with that, she sat back.

I looked back over the courtroom. The clock in the back said we had been going for three hours. Over the course of the time it had taken to conduct this hearing, the parties for the next hearing had waited two hours for their turn before the bar. The municipal judge, a friend of mine, had stepped in the back of the courtroom during the first minutes of the hearing and had stayed through the entire trial. The attorney on the hearing coming up had also waited patiently. Much as I didn't want to keep them all waiting longer, I needed a few minutes to deliberate further, although I had written notes and was mostly ready to say what needed to be said. Still, I assured them I would be gone only ten minutes, and I stuck by that estimate. When I returned, here was my decision:

THE JUDGMENT

As to the matter of the Counterclaim, I find the following facts:

1. Plaintiff Smith materially disregarded the lease by removing and replacing fixtures throughout the house she leased from the Defendant, by damaging walls in multiple dozens of places and by committing haphazard abuse involving doors, carpets and plumbing, all of which resulted in damage exceeding normal wear and tear for a mere ten months occupancy.
2. There is no merit to Plaintiff's claims of various safety issues or to Plaintiff's claims of mold infestation or plumbing defects.
3. Defendant was instead damaged by Plaintiff through lack of maintenance, uninstalling and dismantling of fixtures, damage to walls requiring total repainting of the house, water damage to the kitchen ceiling, and other damage.
4. Defendant's testimony of costs totals $21,880.00. The Court finds this testimony credible except for Defendant's claim of lost rents. The Court finds that the landlord accepted the tenant's abandonment as surrender and that therefore, according to our state law, the rental agreement was

"terminated by the landlord as of the date the landlord has notice of the abandonment." Consequently, Defendant's right to retain prepaid rent and his claims to be owed lost rents for the remaining six months of the 18-month lease, are weighed against his obligation under the law to make "reasonable efforts to rent it at a fair rental." The Court finds that Mr. Jones is entitled to retain rents only from July and August of this year, but that the remaining prepaid rent and the six months claimed as lost rents must be deducted from Mr. Jones's Counterclaim, since there is no way to determine what future period will constitute reasonable time to seek to re-rent the property.

5. Defendant's claim is therefore reduced by $12,950.00.

On the Defendant's Counterclaim the Court renders Judgment in favor of the Defendant and orders that the Plaintiff pay the Defendant $9,010.00.

Williams had not asked for attorney fees in her bottom line figure, but testimony had established that she was entitled to them by contract. After everything I had heard, I was more than a little inclined to include Xena Williams's fees in the Judgment, and I asked her to submit an Affidavit to establish what they would be. There wasn't a peep from Beth Smith when I told her I would advise her of the figure and then include it in the amount she would owe.

Smith's face as she picked up her things and stalked out of the courtroom, however, hid nothing of her opinions. She was the injured party here, first by the landlord and now by the Court. Everybody was against her. Everybody lied. After all, didn't we realize she had been through a terrible divorce?

19

FINDERS KEEPERS

Every once in a while a case is a no brainer from the second it is filed—not necessarily to the parties, but to the Judge. Under most circumstances, the Court cannot refuse to accept a filing though even the clerk in looking at the Complaint knows instantly that it has no chance of success. I must be impartial of course, and occasionally the evidence presented in court entirely changes the impression left by the initial pleadings. Nevertheless, at times I know exactly what is going to happen, and it does.

THE PLEADINGS

Roberta Smith filed a Claim and Delivery action with the Court alleging that her husband Van Jones, from whom she was separated, had in his possession two GPS units that belonged to her. (Roberta Smith was really Roberta Jones, but we'll assume that Smith was her maiden name to keep the parties straight.) According to the Affidavit and Complaint, "I had an investigator install two GPS units on my husband's truck to track him for adultery." Apparently he had discovered and removed the units and she wanted them back. Cost: $750.00 each. In a Claim and Delivery, if the property is "not available," the Court may order a Judgment for the "value thereof." Roberta Smith wanted a Judgment for $1,500.00 if she couldn't get the units themselves.

Jones was quickly served and the hearing was held within fifteen days. He didn't have to file any sort of Answer, just show up to avoid an Order of Dispossession.

THE EVIDENCE

Roberta Smith was a woman of no more than forty years of age. She was accompanied by a gentleman about the same age whom

I believed was probably her private investigator, and I was correct. At the other table sat Van Jones, a man of sixty or more. A woman of eighty or so, who appeared to be his mother (no one ever identified her), sat beside him. I thought the May-December marriage to be a bit odd from the beginning, and I wondered what difficulties between them, beside their generation gap, were responsible for their pending divorce. Since that question was irrelevant, however, I didn't try to find out.

Plaintiff

Mrs. Smith called her private investigator first to testify. P.I. Bryan Green kept it short and sweet. Smith had hired him to investigate her husband, Van Jones, for evidence of adultery. He had attached a GPS tracking device (he kept them in stock) to Jones's 1997 Chevy truck. A few days later the device gave its last ping, locating it in Jones's driveway, and then it went dead. Green followed Jones to a parking lot a day or so later, looked for the device and saw that it had been removed. As his contract with Smith stated he would do, he billed her for the missing device at that point. She agreed to the attachment of another, and Green put another GPS on the truck. The same thing happened another week or so later, and Green billed Smith for the second device. Upon losing the second GPS, Smith filed the Claim and Delivery.

Smith had no more witnesses, and wouldn't herself have testified had I not wished to ask her a question.

I asked Smith who the truck belonged to. She said it was marital property, but in answer to my further question, she said the truck was titled in her husband's name.

That was all Smith had to say, and Jones very promptly and bluntly said he had no questions for her. I turned to Jones and asked if he had anything to say in defense. Actually, he didn't need to say anything, but he appeared to want to.

Defendant

Jones said first that the truck was not marital property. He owned it before they were married and yes, it was in his name.

Second, he said, he knew she was tracking him because she had threatened to do so.

Third, he didn't know where the GPS units were. He denied removing them. Smith was stifling a disbelieving laugh over at her table. Jones added that if he knew where they were, she could have them.

Was there anything else, I asked. No. That was all.

I suggested that Smith, if she wanted to ask any questions, direct them to me and I would then ask Jones. This seems a bit silly, sometimes, but I have found that extremely contentious parties fight less in court if I ask them to follow this procedure, and they actually seem to appreciate not having to look directly at the other party. Smith wanted to know why the GPS units' last pings were from Jones's driveway if he didn't remove and disable them there. That was a bit argumentative, so I rephrased. "Mr. Jones, Mrs. Smith's evidence showed that the last pings of the units were from your driveway. Do you have a response to that, in light of your testimony that you did not remove them?" He did not.

Neither side had anything more, and it was my turn to bring this little hearing to a summary close:

THE JUDGMENT

An old expression has it that possession is nine tenths of the law. That means that in a property dispute, in the absence of clear and compelling testimony or documentation to the contrary, the person in actual possession of the property is presumed to be the rightful owner. In today's case, the facts are clear:

1. Roberta Smith purchased the GPS devices through her private investigator once they went missing.
2. Roberta Smith contracted with her investigator to place the GPS devices on her husband's vehicle, which Green could do by law.
3. Van Jones is the titled owner of the vehicle.

4. The preponderance of the evidence indicates that Van Jones found, disabled and either retained or disposed of the GPS devices.

5. Smith demanded the return of the devices from Jones and was denied.

The Court sees only one reason Smith had any claim to the devices, namely that she paid for them. By her subsequent actions, however, she abandoned any right to the devices. She had them installed without permission on her husband's car, thus leaving them in and attached to his personal property. Jones obviously did not give permission or ask for the devices to be attached. Once the GPS units were left on his personal property, he had no responsibility under law to give them up or over to anyone. Smith might as well have wrapped them up and tied a bow around them.

Under these circumstances, I cannot find any theory of law supporting the Plaintiff's demand. The bottom line: finders keepers. The Complaint is dismissed.

Mr. Jones left the courtroom promptly. Without my saying so, Smith and her P.I. remained at their table. After Jones had exited, Smith—who seemed perfectly understanding about the outcome of her case—wanted to tell me first that her husband had in fact committed adultery—which I didn't need to know—and she asked me if her having GPS units installed would jeopardize her divorce proceeding. Her P.I. was shaking his head, reassuring her it would not, while I simply said I could not weigh in on the matter.

Oddly enough, she thanked me before turning to go. Her pocketbook was $1,500.00 lighter and had not been replenished today. It was just one more cost of divorce.

20

CAN'T TAKE NO FOR AN ANSWER

Occasionally a non-prevailing party in a civil case will appeal the magistrate's judgment or the jury's decision. Out of about 1,800 civil cases I handle in a year, perhaps two are appealed. Most people who file complaints in magistrate court and who do not prevail at trial go away disappointed but they try to put things behind them and move on. But then there is that exceptional person who is doggedly determined to get what he wants.

THE PLEADINGS

Leroy Smith filed a Summons and Complaint against Shanda Jones, board chairman of his former employer, the Community Food Bank, for back wages from the last month he worked at the charitable organization before it ceased operations for lack of funds. Randall Johnson for Defendant Jones filed an Answer and Counterclaim stating that Smith had already filed the same claim in another court and had lost. The Counterclaim asked for damages for Jones's being forced to defend herself yet again and for punitive damages to deter further filings.

Each side submitted further pleadings as the war of words heated up over several months. First, Smith filed a Motion to Dismiss the Counterclaim on the basis of its lacking a signature page and being in an improper form. Smith was being extremely picky. Furthermore, as a *pro se* party, Smith was doing his best to imitate a lawyer but was out of his element. His filings were full of bad grammar, awkward phraseology and logical fallacies. Some irony appeared as well. In supporting his motion to dismiss the Counterclaim on technicalities, Smith quoted the Frivolous Civil Proceedings Sanction Act, a portion of which speaks to the matter of unsigned pleadings. The rest of the Act, however, was about to come back to bite him.

Finally, in his motion to dismiss the Counterclaim, Smith stated his intention to appeal "should the matter of a Counterclaim not be dismissed." The Court always appreciates a good dose of threatening language thrown in to persuade it.

Randall Johnson for the Defendant held his tongue and sent a signature page, inadvertently omitted from the Answer and Counterclaim, with an expressed hope that the Court would accept it as completing the filing in good form. I did, and we proceeded to set a bench trial on the matter.

Johnson then wrote to request a jury trial. I'm always curious about the request for a jury trial. Sometimes it's a tactic between attorneys to promote settlement. Sometimes it's a standard part of certain kinds of claims, such as automobile accidents, where attorneys want to play to juries on which half or more of the people must have had auto accidents and might be putty for a powerful closing argument—one way or the other. But occasionally I wonder if the jury trial request is motivated by some specific hesitation about going before a particular magistrate. The reasons must be well kept secrets, because I haven't arrived at a definitive answer.

At any rate, I wrote to Johnson informing him that because of the new policy of our Supreme Court, a jury trial case in this civil matter would have to be submitted first to mediation, a process I would have no control over as to the time it would take to handle it. A week or so later Johnson filed another document with the Court, a thick sheaf of papers outlining a Motion for Summary Judgment. I could rule on the Motion before sending the case to mediation.

The Summary Judgment motion argued on several levels:

1. Smith seeks unpaid back wages and penalties from Jones, yet Jones was not Smith's employer: the Food Bank was, and the Food Bank is no longer in existence.
2. Smith previously sued the Food Bank over the same issues and the case was dismissed with prejudice (supporting documents were included).

3. Smith also previously sued Jones personally in another court over the same issues after losing the suit against the Food Bank. That suit also was dismissed. (Copies of the judicial dismissal in that case were included. The dismissal in that case was actually a procedural move and did not result from a hearing on the merits.)
4. Even when Jones was a board member of the Food Bank, she had immunity from such lawsuits under state law.

I gave Smith the opportunity to argue against the Motion for Summary Judgment and then I granted it. From everything I had seen, Smith simply did not have any cause for action. But Jones certainly had cause for a further step, and in his motion for Summary Judgment he had taken that step: "Defendant further asks the Court to hold a hearing on the issue of sanctions against the Plaintiff for having brought this lawsuit frivolously."

Upon my entering Summary Judgment on the Complaint in favor of his client, I wrote to both parties indicating that while the Complaint was now disposed, the Counterclaim was still on the table, as was the Motion for Sanctions. Under the Rules of Magistrate Court, if it could stand on its own, the Counterclaim would have to be heard. Since the jury trial request was still in effect, the Counterclaim would have to go to mediation.

Johnson for Defendant Jones promptly submitted a letter to me withdrawing the request for a jury trial. Since the Motion for Sanctions was yet to be heard, the Court set a date for that matter first.

In a day or so, I received a letter from Plaintiff Smith and an attached document titled Notice of Appeal. It was in reference to the Summary Judgment for Defendant just decided. The notice stated that Smith "gives notice of intention to appeal the judgment of in [sic] the above action." It was not the standard boilerplate form and it was not a sufficient document. Smith had not filed an actual appeal with the Court of Common Pleas and he had not stated any reasons for his appeal of the magistrate's decision, which court rules require. His Notice of Appeal was simply a statement that he intended to appeal—at what point, I didn't know. The Notice was not, therefore, the Notice of Appeal required to be served on the magistrate when an actual appeal is filed with the Circuit Court.

I believed that Smith intended to wait until after the hearing on sanctions and perhaps until after disposition of the Counterclaim and then file his appeal when it was all over. His self-study of the law, however, had apparently not resulted in his knowing that he had thirty days to file an appeal—thirty days, in this case, not from the disposition of the Counterclaim, but thirty days from the Summary Judgment. The hearing on sanctions was going to be more than a month distant, and the Counterclaim even farther out. Time would run out for Smith's appeal, and having no duty to help him make more pointless work for me, I didn't intend to tell him so.

SANCTIONS HEARING

Just a day or two prior to the hearing on the motion for sanctions I received a final filing from Defendant Jones, a document showing that in addition to his various suits for back wages, Smith had first of all filed a complaint with the State Department of Labor. The document, a certified copy of the findings of the Department of Labor, had dismissed Smith's complaint. (Interestingly, the Department of Labor was the only party to review Smith's actual complaint about wages. All his subsequent suits were dismissed for other reasons, all valid.)

Defendant

At the hearing, Johnson for Defendant Jones briefly outlined his argument for sanctions. It was mostly a repetition of the defense he presented in his Answer to the original Complaint, but he began with the new bit of evidence he had entered into pleadings.

"First your honor, the Plaintiff filed a complaint with the State Department of Labor and was denied. Next, he sued the

Community Food Bank and he lost. Third, he went after my client, Shanda Jones, because she had been the chairman of the board of the Food Bank, and that case was dismissed. Finally, he filed here, in your court, your honor, trying to take another bite of the apple. He has lost his suit three times over the same issues, and now he has filed here in a desperate attempt to get what he wants. What is to keep him from filing in every court in the county? This is a classic case of frivolous proceedings."

Adding just one more nail to his case, Johnson showed the Court a document confirming that his client Shanda Jones was a material witness in the upcoming trial of the State v. Leroy Smith, in which Smith had been charged with pilfering from the Food Bank while he was an employee. Johnson argued that Smith had filed suit against Jones in part to dissuade her from testifying or to take vengeance on her for it.

I asked Leroy Smith if he would like to argue against the motion.

Plaintiff

Smith began to describe his days at the Food Bank and how Jones had cheated him—and I interrupted him.

"Mr. Smith, the Motion for Summary Judgment was previously granted. I ruled on the Complaint on the basis of what was already in the Pleadings. I realize you are still very passionate about the nature of your Complaint, but because I have granted the Motion for Summary Judgment in favor of the Defendant, the Complaint is done with. The Counterclaim is outstanding, but what we are here for today is the motion to declare that the Complaint was a frivolous proceeding. Certain sanctions proceed from that. Do you understand that?

Smith nodded that he did, and he said that he guessed he didn't have any argument, that he would do what the Court said. I was really a bit surprised by that compliant attitude, though it was a bit defeatist in tone, but I repeated my invitation to hear from him on the motion. He didn't have anything to say. I guess his online legal studies didn't prepare him for making forceful, voluminous arguments in the face of overwhelming odds on the basis of the slimmest of facts—the way any self respecting attorney would do (and to my genuine admiration, I might add). Smith sat down.

I retired for a few minutes to deliberate. Ultimately I drafted a two page order that was essentially a rehearsal of the major arguments of Randall Johnson on behalf of his client, supporting my conclusions: that Plaintiff Smith knew or should have known from his evident self study of the law applying to his case that his suit was not reasonable; that he should have known that he did not have any adequate theory of law under which he could recover from Jones; and that Plaintiff's lawsuit was made "primarily for a purpose other than that of securing the proper discovery, joinder of parties or adjudication of the claim upon which the proceedings are based" [*This language is from the State statutes on frivolous proceedings.*] I also threw in a concern of the Court that Smith had reason to want to make life difficult for Jones because of her prospective testimony in the criminal case upcoming against him.

To end the matter that day, however, I wanted to sum things up for Mr. Smith in plain English to see if I could break through his fervent obsession with pestering Jones about his not getting his last paycheck.

Mr. Smith, it appears that you do not know how to take No for an answer. The Department of Labor told you No. The first court, where you filed against the Food Bank told you No. The second court, where you filed against Shanda Jones told you No. This is the fourth place you have come with the same complaint. In my decision on Summary Judgment I told you No. When you have been told No three times, shopping for a judge who will tell you yes is an abuse of the legal process, and it ends here. Your suit in this Court is a prime example of a frivolous proceeding, and I declare it to be so. You will pay Shandra Jones's legal costs incurred in defending herself against this suit so far. Should she maintain her Counterclaim against you, she will absorb her own costs to press that claim.

In addition, I regret to inform you of another No. After

Summary Judgment was granted to the Defendant on the Complaint, you filed a document titled "Notice of Appeal" in which you stated your intent to appeal the Summary Judgment. You did not file the appeal, however, or serve me with an actual Notice of Appeal and copy of that appeal. You may be wondering if you can now file that appeal. The answer is No. You had thirty days to appeal, and your time has expired.

Defendant's legal costs to date, according to Johnson's affidavit, amounted to $1,750.00. To his credit, Leroy Smith did not argue with the order but merely asked if he could have some time to pay. I asked Johnson what he thought was reasonable. In a generous spirit, Johnson asked the Court to include in its order a directive that Smith be given up to ninety days to pay. I concurred, and Smith seemed relieved.

COUNTERCLAIM

I gave the parties a brief cooling off period following the Sanctions hearing. Actually, I thought it possible that between them Ms. Jones and her attorney might decide not to pursue the Counterclaim, which after all was mostly a quest for punitive damages—rarely awarded in magistrate courts—the prospect for the payment of which was realistically very slim.

Jones did not drop the counterclaim. Furthermore, on the appointed day for the hearing in the Counterclaim, Leroy Smith did not appear. I was not entirely surprised. Smith had behaved respectfully to the Court on his previous appearance, but from the totality of the circumstances surrounding his string of lawsuits, I strongly suspected that Smith was able to put on a good show for the Court or anyone else. Whether on this hearing day he sat at home seething or was absent out of indifference, he obviously didn't believe he would prevail against the counterclaim and he decided to take his chances on what I might do in the way of an award to Jones.

Jones's attorney had subpoenaed several witnesses including

another attorney who had just appeared before me in circuit court preliminary hearings the previous week. That attorney, an assistant solicitor by the name of Reid Williams, without discussing the present case at all, had told me at prelims that he would be seeing me next week and said he hoped that the matter would finally be put to rest. I shared his sentiments.

All the witnesses, including Reid, were now prepared to tell me the story of how Leroy Smith had made Shanda Jones's life a living hell for the past two years. But when Smith did not show for the hearing, I granted default judgment on the counterclaim to Jones and the witnesses were dismissed, save one who had testimony as to damages.

Attorney Randall Johnson called Ms. Jones to the stand. It was the first time I had heard from her. I had granted summary judgment on her complaint and sanctions against Smith for a frivolous action, and neither had involved any testimony from Jones. When she began to speak I realized how timid and emotionally fragile this woman was. Her involvement with the food bank was clearly due to her having a compassionate heart and tender disposition. It would not be difficult to imagine the effect that a series of lawsuits had had on her.

Under questioning, Jones talked about how Mr. Smith's lawsuits brought sudden terror into her life. She had never been sued before that time and she was totally unnerved. She didn't know how to go about getting a lawyer and she didn't have the money for one anyway. When finally she was put in touch with the local legal services organization, the man who eventually became her attorney was asked to take the case against the food bank *pro bono.* Then the personal lawsuits against Jones were filed, as well as against another board member, who was the other witness who stayed for this hearing. Jones told how her husband was in the hospital in a coma during the time Smith was pursuing her with his litigation. I wanted to know if she had any reason to believe that Smith knew about her husband. She said it had been in all the papers how her husband had been hit by a pickup truck while retrieving litter from the road. She believed Smith knew and meant to cause her distress by compounding her problems.

Jones had also missed a considerable amount of work. An employee of a local cancer center, she was paid $18.00 per hour and had missed about 28 hours. Her actual damages for lost wages were $500.00. What she deserved to be compensated in actual damages for emotional pain and suffering was not argued specifically by Attorney Johnson. While I had been deliberately holding in abeyance any estimation of a figure, I was beginning to develop a clear impression of this woman's distress.

I remembered clearly how when I was a much younger man I had been shocked by a lawsuit filed against me and my wife over a car accident she had. It kept us up nights and gave me a sinking feeling of impending doom. I don't know that I would have claimed that I had "pain and suffering," however. That's another matter. Some people's claims of suffering are patently bogus; others' claims are real but exaggerated; but Jones's claims, I was beginning to believe, were altogether substantiated by the facts as I knew them already and by her testimony taking place.

Randall Johnson asked Jones if she were asking for the statutory limit of $7,500.00 in actual and punitive damages. She was.

The witness who remained for the hearing, a Mr. Gary Green, now testified. He had reason to believe he would be the next person to be sued. His position with the board made him an emotional target of Smith. He believed that punitive damages were advisable in this case in order to dissuade Smith from suing anyone ever again over his claims.

The Defense rested. I asked Attorney Johnson if he would like to sum up his case. He smiled and said he could if I wanted him to. In fact, I said, I hoped he would. I wanted to know specifically how he saw the counterclaim for punitive damages, as distinguished from actual ones, as being different from the sanctions already imposed on Mr. Smith—sanctions were punitive as well. How did he view the difference to Ms. Jones? Johnson argued that of course the sanctions resulted in the reimbursement of Jones for her attorney costs—his bills, in other words. The punitive award would go to Jones. The difference lay in the mere fact that the statute allowed Jones to be awarded punitive damages if justified, in addition to Smith's being required to pay the bill for the legal costs, if sanctioned. In fact, Randall Johnson said, he believed it was fitting and proper that the Court should award the additional, punitive damages precisely because in my ruling I had already ordered sanctions on the same arguments as Johnson was making today about Smith's abuse of process in filing the string of lawsuits.

I did not disagree. I had not asked Johnson for his justification in order to settle the issue for me, but in order to hear him parse the matter from a legal standpoint and display for me how he saw the difference. Call it professional curiosity on my part.

Johnson sat down. I pondered a moment and scribbled some numbers. Originally, I thought I might arrive at this point and announce that I would deliberate overnight. I found that to be unnecessary under the circumstances. I also thought it was fitting to bring a conclusion to this entire matter here and now by rendering judgment.

JUDGMENT

The Court's having previously found the Plaintiff's complaint frivolous and having imposed sanctions against him for attorney fees, and the Court's having granted default Judgment today to the Defendant in the matter of the Counterclaim, I find the actual damages suffered by the Defendant to be $500.00 for lost wages and $2,000 for pain and suffering. In addition, I award the Defendant $5,000.00 in punitive damages, for the maximum award in this Court of $7,500.00.

The gavel came down. I really hoped it was finally over—for Shanda Jones, for this witness and former board member, Gary

Green, and for me. I was really tired of seeing this case coming back across my desk.

Of course, it wasn't over for Leroy Smith. He started out suing everyone in sight for unpaid wages, which he had calculated on his Complaint in this way:

"$1,200.00 per week x 3 (the full amount) = $3,600.00 x 2 weeks in the rear = $7,200."

That was his actual statement, word for word, whatever it may have meant. We had, I hoped, arrived at the end of the saga, and I hoped Mr. Smith now had some wages coming in, because he was facing $9,250.00 in sanctions and judgments out of my court and who knows what in the way of fines or jail if he were convicted in the criminal charges pending against him. His inability to take No for an answer had come back to bite him—in the rear.

21

THE PRICE OF LYING TO THE JUDGE

Most civil cases, as someone has said, are just honest differences of opinion between honest people about money. In my experience, that description is generally true, but notable exceptions crop up with regularity. Honesty may be the best policy, but it is occasionally not the policy chosen by either a defendant or a plaintiff—or both. On the criminal side of my work, defendants more than occasionally lie. I had one fellow caught in a solicitation of prostitution sting who claimed with a straight face that he was only trying to hire the female police officer decoy to clean his house. Defendants in criminal cases lie about being sick, poor, injured, indisposed, or otherwise unable to have taken care of legal obligations, or prevaricate about how utterly destroyed their lives will be to have to pay restitution or a stiff fine. On the civil side, plaintiffs sometimes construct elaborate claims to try to recoup money they spent foolishly on risks they took ill-advisedly. Defendants sometimes simply play dumb about all complaints against them even when the tactic makes them appear unbelievably naive. The dishonesty of parties must be successful now and then when the liars are practiced, and no doubt the Court never knows in those cases that it has been duped.

When, however, the Court finds out it has been lied to, whether by an opportunistic plaintiff or an evasive defendant, it does not sit well with the Judge. The following Claim and Delivery case started out in the typical fashion. Then the Court caught the defendant in a lie.

THE PLEADINGS

Smith Finance Company filed a Claim and Delivery action against Jamar Jones over a loan for a little more than $300.00 that Jones had taken out three months before, on which he had never made any payments. Jones had put up three pieces of property as collateral: a printer-scanner, a digital projector, and a DVD player, totaling $800.00 in value. Smith Finance wanted the property.

Jamar Jones was not required to submit an answer, only to show up for court if he wished to be heard on why the property should not be dispossessed. The Court hears such C&Ds weekly or more frequently. One out of three times the defendant does not appear, and two out of three times defendants do appear, they have no real defense against the action, and an Endorsement of Dispossession is signed. As far as the hearing was concerned, this case largely appeared no different.

THE EVIDENCE

Plaintiff

Rhonda Smith represented Smith Finance Company and rattled off the basic testimony against Jones, a young man about twenty-five years old, who did appear and sat quietly at the defendant's table. Smith Finance had lent Jamar Jones $333.93 for a seven month term and had accepted as collateral Jones's three items as reported. Jamar had never made a payment. At the time Smith filed with the Court, she said Jamar's payoff would have been $502.98, an amount that included the stiff interest on such high risk loans as well as the filing fee. Smith Finance simply wanted the property. Rhonda Smith said she believed they could sell it and break even.

Often when I have small finance companies before me as plaintiffs, I ask them about the details of their contracts. On this occasion I looked at the "Truth-In-Lending Disclosure Statement" and asked if the monthly payments were to be $60.00. Yes. And was the Annual Percentage Rate 73.02%? Yes. (Our state does not cap interest rates. I find such rates outrageous, but the fact is that other businesses such as payday lenders charge fees which, if extrapolated to annual percentage rates, would be phenomenally higher than even 73%.) So, I asked if, for the amount of his loan, $333.93, Jamar would be paying $86.07 in interest over seven months. Yes.

Jones had no questions of Smith. I turned to Jones.

Defendant

Jamar Jones had, he said, been dismissed from his job at a nearby church shortly after taking out the loan. I knew of the church. I had grown up attending it. Jones went on to say that he had been unjustly accused of a crime, which he didn't specify, and that the church had dismissed him for this cause. Before he could fill in the details, I told Jamar that I didn't need to know about that matter in this context, that I didn't know whether or not it was a matter that would come before me, and that it didn't appear relevant to this particular civil case. He went on, saying that he had a line on a job but hadn't gotten it yet, and simply had not had the money to pay Smith Finance.

This sort of "defense" is what I hear about 90% of the time. Insufficient as it is to counter the Plaintiff's complaint or prevent judgment in the Plaintiff's favor, it is emblematic of the hard economic times many people find themselves in.

Jones went on to tell me that he had recently been evicted from his apartment, the address of which he gave, which informed me that his was an eviction case that had gone through my court. This had taken place not more than two or three weeks before. Jones said "you," meaning court authorities, had come out to the apartment and all his possessions had been removed.

I said, "So you were 'set out'? Your possessions were put out by the roadway?" Yes, he said. He lost a sofa, chairs, everything. As difficult a thing as this is for the court to do, it must be done and is done quite often. It's the only way some people will get the message that they aren't going to live in their landlord's house or apartment rent-free anymore.

I asked Jones where he was living, and he said here and there, wherever he could find to stay. I was curious about the picture this created in my mind. Jamar conjured up an image of his standing by and watching the Constable of my court oversee the removal of all his belongings and their placement by the road. At the apartment complex where Jamar lived at the time, that meant beside the internal parking lot. According to his description, he implied that he then wandered around looking for a place to stay. Jones also implied that he didn't get to take *anything* he owned to wherever it was that he bunked down night after night for the past two weeks. He repeated that he lost "sofa, chairs, everything."

So, I wanted to know specifically, do you have the DVD player, the projector and the printer-scanner? No. It's all gone, he said.

Neither party had anything more to add.

THE JUDGMENT

The decision in this case seemed simple. Faced with similar circumstances, I usually grant a judgment on the spot for the monetary value of the property, though frequently I realize that the plaintiff may never be made whole this way. After all, the parties are in court because the defendant can't pay back a loan. If he can't pay back the loan, he won't be able to pay a judgment. Often, debtors don't own anything that could be seized and sold, either. That's why creditors want the property put up as collateral.

Something about the testimony bothered me, however. Instead of issuing a judgment order for the money, I decided the case this way:

> Mr. Jones, you admit to the facts the Plaintiff complains of. My Judgment is in therefore in favor of the Plaintiff. I am going to sign an Order of Dispossession, which means that the Plaintiff has the right to come and take possession of the property listed as collateral, under the supervision of the Constable and the authority of the Court. [Normally, the clerk sets a date for the pick-up right then, before the parties leave the courtroom. That date may be a few days afterward.]
>
> You've told me that you do not have the property anymore, so this Order is something of a technicality. But what I'm going to do is to send my Constable to verify that the property cannot be had—he'll go to where you're staying right now—and when

he has verified that fact, I will give the Plaintiff a Judgment for the value of the property, which is $800.00.

I know you won't be able to pay that Judgment right now, but you say you're about to get a job, so I want to encourage you to take care of this debt as soon as possible to avoid the problems it can cause if it remains outstanding.

To the Plaintiff:

Ms. Smith, I'm giving you a copy of an Affidavit of Non-Availability. That's a form to be filled in and sworn to, saying that the property the Court has ordered to be given to you is not available. You will go with the Constable when he goes to where Mr. Jones stays. Once you have verified that the three pieces of property cannot be had, I will give you the Judgment for the monetary value.

As I left the courtroom, the clerk was getting the address where Jamar Jones was staying. It was the address we had on the case file. Consequently, it was the residence over which the Court had jurisdiction for an order of Dispossession.

The clerk hurriedly returned to the office, and before the parties had left the courtroom and lobby, she told me that the address was Jamar's mother's house—he had moved back home. I knew there was no way he had left those three, valuable, very portable pieces of property sitting outside for the vultures to pick over after he had been set out. Either he had a car or someone else did, and he had taken those things to his mother's house. What happened next confirmed my suspicions.

I ordered the Constable to go with the Plaintiff immediately to the Defendant's mother's home and execute the order. If the items were not there, so be it. The clerk told Jamar that the Constable would be going to his mother's house right away.

Jamar hurried off into a corner of the lobby and furiously keyed in a number to his cell phone. The Constable exited the rear of the court building to go to his car. The Plaintiff paused until Jamar was off the phone and then she rushed off to her own vehicle.

The Constable and the Plaintiff met at the mother's address but Jamar didn't show up. Rhonda Smith told the Constable that she heard Jones's side of his cell phone conversation and that Jones wanted his mother to come pick him up and get out of the house and stay away for a while. Clearly, he did not want the Constable gaining entry under Court order, because if he did, he would find that projector, DVD player, and printer-scanner right there in his mother's house.

Jamar Jones lied to me. I had suspected it, but the confirmation was Jones's hurried plan to be absent when the Constable came to call. There simply was no other reason for him or his mother to evade the due process of law.

My Constable called me from the house after he had sat there in his car for thirty minutes waiting for Jamar and his mother to show up. They didn't. What was he to do? The law specifically allows the Constable to make entry by sufficient force, and to call on the "power of his county" if necessary. It was also a workable solution to summon a locksmith to the scene. A fellow constable had advised my man in such circumstances to write a letter and leave a card and see what results that got. In this case, of course, if he didn't sit on the doorstep until Jamar came home, Jamar would have plenty of opportunity that night to take the sought-after property to a friend's house. Realizing that Jamar might win round one, I helped the Constable craft a letter.

The letter told Mr. Jones that the Court had ordered that the property listed was to be surrendered to a creditor and that the law gave the Constable the authority to break the locks and enter. It advised Jamar to cooperate with the Court in turning over the collateral. It gave him a time when the Constable would come to pick up the property. It also reminded Jones that the Court had previously ordered him not to conceal, transfer or destroy the property, and that if he had, he would be ruled into the court to face contempt charges. After finishing the letter, I set it aside briefly.

Meanwhile, curious about Jamar's eviction, which I knew I had not been involved with, other than to sign the routine papers, I looked up his name on the county's public index. Indeed, three weeks before, he had been evicted for non-payment of rent, having never requested a hearing. The Constable had performed the set out. And below the eviction case in our court, the public index listed five criminal charges against Jamar in the municipal court in the past year, three of which had been transferred to the Circuit Court. All five were for giving false information to police. Mr. Jones was a frequent liar.

The Constable took the letter to the house three days later—after a weekend—and promptly called me to report that the mother had answered the door and had instantly gone into a fit of rage. "My boy ain't got that stuff! It ain't here!" She proceeded to call the court, police and the entire "system" every name in the book and generally was anything but cooperative, simply for the Constable's attempting to post the letter. The letter did not make any demand of Jones's mother but only mentioned that Jones had given her address as the place where he was currently living. She was upset, however, merely for being involved in the situation at all. The Constable asked her to speak to me. He believed she would be satisfied only then.

Generally, I don't involve myself this personally in the execution of my orders. That's what I have my own private police officer for. I decided, however, to do so in this case. Jones's mother (I didn't know her name and it was not safe to assume she was "Mrs. Jones") was instantly respectful to me on the phone, but she still vehemently denied that her son lived there, saying that she didn't see eye to eye or shoulder to shoulder or anything else with him, and that she didn't know where he lived. He was homeless for the moment, she said. I asked her to clarify for me whether or not Jamar's collateral was currently in her house, and she immediately and strongly told me it was not. She seemed believable, but I was not satisfied that she was telling the whole truth, given the nature of the phone conversation Rhonda Smith overheard and the absence of both Jones and his mother from the house the previous Friday. With no way to prove she was lying however, I told her to give the phone back to my Constable, and I instructed him to bring the letter back to the courthouse and write off Jones's mother's house as a target.

I re-crafted the letter for mailing to Jamar's post office box—he had divulged its existence after the Claim and Delivery hearing—and this new version of the letter contained all the previous information except that it directed Jones to bring the property to the courthouse by the following Friday. My man mailed the new letter in an unmarked envelope, just in case Jamar was inclined to avoid official correspondence.

The letter did not miss its mark, because Jamar called the office the following Friday, just hours away from the deadline. He wanted to speak to me, which I would not do at this point. He called while I was at lunch, anyway, but the clerk had the impression that he wanted to know exactly what would happen if he were unable to bring the property. The letter, however, had made that matter very clear.

Jamar did not show up with the property by the deadline.

I decided I had enough evidence to bring Jamar Jones before me on a "Rule to Show Cause" as to why the Court should not hold him in contempt for disobeying the order of the Court, the "Order Restraining Damage or Concealment of Property." This basic restraining order is issued in every Claim and Delivery Case. Its intention is to make defendants think twice before they hide, sell or otherwise dispose of that wide screen TV rather than let the finance company take it. Quite candidly I suspect that more than half the time, the order is ignored. Unfortunately there isn't much way of proving that. Usually the story is, "Your honor, we had a break-in and that TV got stolen." No, they didn't make a report for whatever reason—so the story can't be checked out.

At any rate, I issued the Rule to Show Cause and set a date for a hearing. Further, I had the Rule served with an accompanying Subpoena, personally delivered by the Constable. He had to sit on the porch a few hours later to serve it. My reason for doing things this way was that now Mr. Jones would face the possibility of contempt of court for two causes: first for disobeying the Order Restraining Damage or Concealment," and then for disobeying a Subpoena to appear, if he didn't show up. If he did not appear for the hearing, I would find him in contempt for that, and by failing to appear he would be found in contempt on the original order. Jamal would be facing two consecutive 30-day sentences. I doubted he wanted to visit the jail that much.

The solution Jamal Jones would then have would be first to comply with the Order of Dispossession and allow the Constable access to retrieve the collateral property. That would dispose of the contempt citation on the Restraining Order. Then he would have to go to jail for 30 days for contempt of court for not obeying a lawful subpoena—though, if he complied with the surrender of the property, I would probably suspend sentence on the rest.

Jamal did not show for the hearing. I issued a bench warrant for his arrest on contempt. He was picked up within the week. He was in jail less than forty-eight hours when his mother called the court with the surprise discovery of the property being sought. She turned it over to the Constable that day, and I immediately sent a get-out-of-jail-free card to the county detention center.

It would have been so much easier to comply with the order of the Court to begin with. Even more, it would have been a much better policy to be honest with the judge. I really, really don't like to discover I've been lied to.

22

OUT OF MY JURISDICTION

A program presenter at a magistrate's meeting spoke about a situation that might come up in our courts, involving a person wanting to sue the Post Office. Considering what many people think about the Post Office, I imagine the desire to sue comes up much more often than an actual case is filed, but I digress. Anyway, the presenter said that the Magistrate should always inform the complainant that a suit against the Post Office does not lie within the jurisdiction of the Summary Court. If the complainant insists on filing suit anyway, the presenter said to take the filing fee, then hold a hearing on your own motion to dismiss for lack of jurisdiction, and when the plaintiff can't come up with a justification that trumps Federal law, dismiss the suit. The court system will be one filing fee richer and the Magistrate won't encroach on the Federal prerogative.

Some things just don't lie in the jurisdiction of the Magistrate Court. Occasionally, calling on the foundational statutes that lay out jurisdiction is a convenient way to eliminate some of the complications thrust into a matter. A simple Notice to Quit, for instance, turned into a matter the Magistrate had to delay for two jurisdictional issues.

THE PLEADINGS

Plaintiff Richard Smith filed a Notice to Quit against Gerald and Gloria Jones. Smith had bought the Joneses' house at a county tax sale. The sale required Smith to wait a year for the Joneses to redeem the property if they could, but they didn't. As soon as title passed to Smith, he gave the Joneses a month's notice to vacate, and when they didn't, he came to the Court to evict them through the Summary Ejectment of Trespasser action—the Notice to Quit.

So far, the case seemed open and shut, but the Joneses called and asked for a hearing, and when asked by the clerk to submit an Answer, they did. In the Answer, Mrs. Jones stated:

> "My name was forged on the letter by my son and I did not get or see certified letter. The sheriff's office is investigating the signature. I need an extinction to stay here until I talk with a lawyer!"

Pretty obviously (and this was confirmed at a hearing later), Mrs. Jones meant that the County's letter informing them their house would be sold for the unpaid taxes was somehow intercepted by their son and signed for by him, unbeknownst to them. In other words, their defense would be that they didn't have notice of the tax sale. And of course, they wanted an "extinction" to have time to deal with the matter.

How the Joneses found out about their son's alleged forging of a signature, they didn't say, and I never found out. Nor could I guess why he would want to do so or want to keep his parents from finding out that their home would be sold for the taxes owed. All I had before me was the claim that they didn't have notice. But the Joneses didn't argue that the County didn't send notice, only that their son didn't give the notice to them. Since the County sent notice, it did what it should have done and the tax sale would have been proper. Besides, the Joneses admitted they had not paid the taxes. It wasn't as if they didn't know their default would come back to bite them.

But the issue raised by the Joneses complicated the case, and in the hearing I scheduled, I addressed the matter before taking any testimony on the underlying Notice to Quit.

First, I asked Smith about title to the property. He showed it to me. There was nothing bogus about it, and the Joneses didn't suggest there was. What they contested was not Mr. Smith's right to oust them if he legitimately owned the property: they wanted to contest the legitimacy of the sale in the first place. Because they claimed they had not received notice, they wanted to bring the County into the Court and undo the sale. In other words, they wanted to counterclaim against the County. I am obligated by the Rules of Magistrate Court to construe a defense that amounts to a counterclaim *as* a counterclaim and give the other party a chance to answer it before trying the matter. I had to consider the Joneses' defense as a counterclaim, not against Smith, but against the County. What that would involve would actually be joining the County to the case as a third party defendant.

This raised two issues for me. First, the Magistrate Court is not supposed to hear cases where title to real estate comes into question. If a plaintiff files suit over such an issue and the defendant raises this defense, the Magistrate has a procedure in the law to follow to get the case into the higher court. Second, joining the County to the case as a third party defendant for any reason would embroil the Magistrate in a conflict of interest, since while he is appointed by the Governor, he is paid by the County. I actually could have joined the County as a third party defendant *if* the other matter about title to real estate had not been an issue, but I would have had to submit the case to the chief magistrate of our County for an out-of-county judge to hear. As I said, sometimes jurisdictional issues thrust a matter into complication.

The case at its heart was really quite simple, however. The Joneses were just two unfortunate people who were trying to get along on very little and had gotten into a hole they weren't going to be able to get out of. I asked if they had seen the lawyer they said they needed to see, but they hadn't. They didn't have the money. After the hearing that day, my clerk would refer them to a free legal service for whatever help that might provide them. Probably what they really needed was just a little time to move out.

I looked at Gerald and Gloria Jones and realized that I couldn't fix their real problem. I could only give them a little time by a legitimate continuance. I was sure that the final result would be they would have to move. If they had any chance to turn back the clock, however, it would be through the complexities of the law, and my order opened up that door of opportunity ever so slightly.

CONTINUATION AND ORDER

First, I continued the case. South Carolina law required that when a defendant says a plaintiff's suit calls title to real estate into question, the defendant must post an undertaking (sign a bond) with the Court and agree that if the plaintiff files the same complaint in the Circuit Court within twenty days, the Defendant will consider himself served with the suit. The Magistrate Court then dismisses the action before it, and the parties can go hash it out before the higher court. The undertaking or bond is simply to protect the interests of the plaintiff. The Court would make certain that the defendant's bond was for enough to cover the plaintiff's claim of damages and court costs.

In this case, it wasn't Plaintiff Smith whose Complaint called into question the title to real estate, but Defendant Jones's Counterclaim against the County, which was not a party to the action. The Joneses were not asking for any damages from the County, but they clearly wanted the sale invalidated and title returned to them. Since there were no damages and the County was not presently a party to the suit, there was no one to require an undertaking from, but I did intend to give them twenty days—actually thirty-two (thirty days landed on a Saturday)—to file their suit against the County.

I did not actually expect them to sue the County. I knew they would have to get a lawyer to do it, and knowing what the nature of their counterclaim was, I was certain a lawyer would not take the case. But if by some stretch they did go file a claim against the County, my complying with the statute would allow me to dismiss their counterclaim from my Court and let the Circuit Court deal with it, which I was certain they would do with dispatch.

Other than providing for this unlikely action on their part, what this continuation would do was give the Joneses a few days to get their things together and find another place to live.

After I gave them leave to consult an attorney and file suit against the County, I then instructed the parties that if suit were not filed by the Defendants in the Circuit Court in thirty-two days, we would return to my Court the following day and I would dismiss the counterclaim on jurisdictional grounds. Then I would hear any defense the Joneses had against the Notice to Quit, other than the claim that the County's sale had been invalid. The Joneses had asserted no other defense and none was suggested by anything they said at the first hearing. When we met again, the issue before the Court would be back to the open and shut case it was to begin with. In thirty-two days, the Joneses would be given a twenty-four hour notice to be gone.

Opponents of property taxes sometimes argue that in America we don't actually own our property anymore; we just rent it from counties. Whether that argument is solid or not is for another court to decide, but obviously it's a fact of life in most places that if you don't pay your property taxes, your land along with its improvements will get sold out from under you, often for a ridiculously small sum. By the time an eviction resulting from a tax sale gets to my court, the underlying matter is out of my hands. My sad duty is to enforce the law and give the new owner the big ticket item he paid a few bucks for. Sometimes life is tough and the Court's order unavoidable.

23

ESTOPPEL!

In learning the language of law, lawyers and judges find out fairly quickly that many of the terms that make up the jargon of their profession come from ancient or obscure sources. An example is "estoppel." In the U.S. this term refers to the *doctrine of equitable estoppel,* which means that a person is precluded from denying or asserting anything contradicting what has been established as truth, either by a court or legislature, or by his own words and actions.

Estoppel is usually presented as a defense. Particularly in attorney-prepared defenses, a defendant may answer a lawsuit by saying that he has documentation showing that the plaintiff is now claiming something that directly and clearly contradicts what he said in a contract or offer. Or, the defense may be that another court has already heard the same matter before the court now, and has decided against the plaintiff's claims. In other words, estoppel means, "He can't do that!"

Some linguistic authorities connect *estoppel* to an obsolete French word, *estoupail,* which means "variation" and is related to the Old French *estopper* meaning to impede. The derivation seems likely but there may have been a bit of officious creativity involved. Lawyers—like doctors, scientists, theologians and others in longstanding professional fields—like to use foreign terms, especially arcane ones, the meanings of which are known mostly to those professionals themselves. After all, what good is it to have professional jargon if everyone else understands it just as well as you do?

Estoppel is actually a very common defense, however, along with "failure to state a claim for which relief can be granted." Quite often, such defenses are piled on for effect, but occasionally one of them is the very thing that goes to the heart of a matter. Such was the case with native Germans Herman Schmidt (I know, all plaintiffs in this book are Smith, but Schmidt is, after all, German for Smith) v. Klaus Johannsen (both the German Johannsen and the Welsh Jones mean "John's son.").

THE PLEADINGS

Schmidt filed suit against Johannsen for $2,000.00. From the oddly worded and badly handwritten Complaint the Court could make out that Johannsen had sued Schmidt in another court in another county over some matter not specified. Schmidt was now suing Johannsen for the same amount, over claims that Johannsen had failed to finish some construction within a six month time frame. It appeared from the Complaint that it was a matter of tit for tat. The Answer mostly addressed the construction issue, as Johannsen said he had no agreement with Schmidt but was rather a consultant for another firm that actually had the contract with Schmidt for construction.

THE EVIDENCE

A hearing was scheduled in the matter, and in preparation for trial the Court determined to question Plaintiff Schmidt first about any contract or oral agreement with Johannsen. If there were no agreement the Court could enforce, this case would be disposed very quickly and the judge could go to lunch early.

In chambers before the trial, the Court's clerk told me that everyone in the courtroom was chattering away heatedly in German. I know some French and a smattering of Spanish, but no German, though I can pronounce some German words just on sight. I hoped they all spoke good English. They did, but apparently they did not have an equally good command of American law.

I began by saying to the Plaintiff that typically one of two things would constitute a Complaint: either the Defendant had done something wrong to the Plaintiff out of the blue, or the Plaintiff and Defendant had a contract with each other and the Plaintiff claimed the Defendant had breached that contract. Which was it, I wanted to know? Schmidt seemed confused, in spite of the very simple statement I had made. I rephrased: "Do you have an agreement with Johannsen that you say he violated?"

The answer was curious: "Pretty much."

I pressed the matter further. "Either you do or you don't. If you don't, there is nothing for the Court to enforce. If you do, it could be an oral agreement or a written one. What kind of agreement do or did you have?"

At that, Schmidt turned to a fellow he had brought with him, name unknown, and the two exchanged rapid words in German. Then Schmidt produced a document. "I have this estimate," he said. "This is what he said he would do."

I instructed him to give the document to the clerk, who showed it to Johannsen. Johannsen didn't object to it as evidence, but merely clarified that the document was an offer. He wanted to speak further but I held up my hand. Schmidt was going to have to do this all on his own for now, and I might never need to hear from Johannsen at all.

"So this is an offer, is that right?"

"Yes, your honor," said Schmidt.

"Did it ever become a contract? Is there a version or copy of this offer that is signed by either party?" I said. I looked at the document as it was handed to me. It was entirely in German, with a couple of paragraphs highlighted.

"No, your honor," said Schmidt.

Knowing that many estimates become contracts by being acted on, acknowledged or accepted in some way, if only by payment of money, I said, "Did you accept this offer in some way? Did you pay Mr. Johannsen—" and I looked down for a figure, and seeing one for $8,750.00, I filled in the blank with that amount.

"I paid him $1,000.00 a month later," he said, and gave me the date. Schmidt had another document in hand, which turned out to be a list of payments printed out from his accounting software. The total amounted to something over $11,000.00. Johannsen didn't object to the evidence.

"And basically what was it that Johannsen agreed to do for this sum of money?" I said. "I see here, highlighted on the offer, Exhibit 1, something about—" and I did my best to pronounce the German words, which, because of some linguistic tips learned long ago, I believed I could do, even though I didn't understand any of it— "die Bauleitung und Mittler zwischen Schmidt, der Bauleitung und den Behoerden. ...Alle geleisteten Stunden werden dokumentiert." I then said, "You may all now laugh at my pronunciation."

Over at Schmidt's table, the unknown person shook his head No, and smiled as if to say that I had actually done well, and he gave me a thumbs up. The German was explained briefly. I was still uncertain about what the entire agreement was, but what I was most interested in knowing was how Johannsen had breached the contract, in Schmidt's view.

"So, Mr. Schmidt," I said, "what we have here is an offer that you accepted by making a payment to Mr. Johannsen within a month or so of the offer (which was sent by email). And in your Complaint you ask for $2,000.00 in damages. What is the $2,000.00 for? Where does that figure come from?"

Schmidt's answer was surprising. He explained that Johannsen had sued him in the neighboring county for $2,000.00 and that he, Schmidt, had been unable to submit an Answer in thirty days. Apparently the suit was over an unpaid invoice for $2,000.00, which Schmidt had not paid because he took issue with Johanssen's work. In a rambling as well as rapid explanation he said that he had left phone messages about the matter (with the other Court, I believe, not Johannsen) that had not been returned. There was a judgment, he wasn't allowed to have a hearing, and he talked to the sheriff, and he was advised that it was too late and that he should just pay the $2,000.00. So he filed against Johanssen in this Court so he could have a hearing.

From this, and looking at the Complaint itself, I gathered that Schmidt had been sued for the unpaid invoice, failed to submit an Answer within the allowed time, and that a Default Judgment had been issued for the $2,000.00. When Schmidt tried to call the Court to explain things, the Court didn't argue about the matter.

Smith didn't explain why the sheriff was involved at that point, but the date of the Judgment was more than two years previous, and I later surmised that after waiting a while to collect, Johanssen had applied for Execution Against Property to get paid his Judgment. Probably the sheriff went out to demand either that Schmidt pay the debt or turn over his extra BMW. The sheriff advised him to just pay the Judgment, which Schmidt did. But since he had never gotten the hearing he wanted on the dispute between him and Johannsen—even though that was entirely his own fault—he turned around and sued Johannsen in my Court (Schmidt was in the other Court's jurisdiction and Johannsen was in mine).

"So let me see if I have this right," I said. "Johannsen sued you for an unpaid invoice and got a Default Judgment—" Schmidt was nodding all along— "which you paid, and you filed suit in this Court so you could contest the original matter in a hearing. Is that it?"

"Yes, your honor!" Schmidt said triumphantly, as if my understanding exactly what the case was about constituted a giant leap toward his soon prevailing.

"So this suit is about the same matter as the one Mr. Johannsen filed against you? —the dispute over whether or not he had performed some of the contracted work to your satisfaction?" I asked.

"Yes!"

"Did you file an appeal with the other court?" I asked. Schmidt consulted his friend and then said no.

"Did you file a Motion for Relief from Judgment?" I asked, "on grounds of mistake or excusable neglect?" I believed strongly that he wouldn't know about such motions, but it didn't matter. My point was to find out if he had done anything at all to try to get a review of the matter in the other court. Again, he said no.

"Did you consult an attorney?" I added finally. That part he understood completely, and he said no, seeming to sense defeat.

"So," I continued, "You sued to get your $2,000.00 back?"

"Yes!" he said, with a little return of his anticipation of getting to argue his case.

So, it was a matter of tit for tat after all. I sat for a moment thinking to myself that I didn't believe I remembered ever having a case where someone sued merely to get back money the other had won in a previous suit over the same issue—dollar for dollar.

THE JUDGMENT

"Mr. Schmidt, it's pretty simple," I said, "You can't do that. We have a principle in American law called *equitable estoppel*—I know that sounds German, but it's not. *Estoppel* means pretty much what it sounds like: Stop! In this case, it means that this matter has already been decided by a court, the one in the neighboring county. You can't sue Mr. Johannsen "back" over the same matter, because it has already been decided. You could have filed an appeal within thirty days, but that time is long since gone. You might have filed a motion for Relief of Judgment, and possibly still could, except that you have already paid the Judgment. If there is anything left to you, I don't know what it would be, but if you have any questions about that you should consult an attorney."

I rapped the gavel perfunctorily, gathered up my papers and rose to retire. Schmidt seemed respectful as I exited the courtroom, but once in the lobby he and Johannsen went at each other in rapid and heated German, which sounded like clearing their throats and spitting as much as anything. A police officer was in the lobby as well, which no doubt prevented the exchange from escalating into something worse. If it hadn't abated shortly, I was prepared to go out there myself and tell them to *"Estoppel it!"*

www.ingramcontent.com/pod-product-compliance
Lightning Source LLC
Chambersburg PA
CBHW031927190326
41519CB00007B/438